PLAYING IN THE GOSPEL

Spiritual & Pastoral Models

Thomas E. Clarke

D1483642

DUQUESNE UNIVERSITY LIBRARY

Playing in the Gospel

Playing in the Gospel
Spiritual and Pastoral Models

Thomas E. Clarke, S.J.

Sheed & Ward

BX 2350.2
C 56
1986

Copyright © 1986
Thomas E. Clarke

All rights reserved. No part of this book may be reproduced or transmitted in any form or by any means, electronic or mechanical, including photocopying, recording or by an information storage and retrieval system without permission in writing from the Publisher.

Sheed & Ward ™ is a service of National Catholic Reporter Publishing, Inc.

ISBN: 1-55612-013-3

Published by: Sheed & Ward
    115 E. Armour Blvd. P.O. Box 414292
    Kansas City, MO 64141

    To order, call: (800) 821-7926

Contents

MAY 29 1987

Introduction

Like many theologians in the past few decades, I have been much attracted by an approach to theological reflection which draws consciously on the notion of *model*. Similarly, I have undergone a major shift in my understanding and practice of theology by paying more attention to experience — my own experience and that of others — especially as this experience finds embodiment in *story*. Out of both of these learnings comes the present book. It reaches back into my personal history of theologizing with the help of several of the models I have used. In each chapter I rehearse for myself and for the reader just how particular notions, distinctions, and frameworks of reflection first came into my life and gave fresh energy and insight to the ways in which I thought, spoke, and wrote about the Gospel.

I am not, however, offering merely an edited collection of talks and articles of the past twenty years. What makes this book different for me and, I hope, for the reader is: First, I situate each model within the story of where and how I first encountered it, in my own Christian imagination, or, often, in the utterance of some other speaker or writer. If there is anything to what has been called "narrative theology," then an adequate grasp of an idea requires that we situate it within the experience that gave it birth. Second, I make a conscious effort to link the models with one another, so that they are seen as interrelated perspectives on what it means to be human and Christian. Third, I engage in this reflection on experience with the purpose of encouraging readers to do the same with their own stories and their own models.

Although I will be proposing some theoretical constructs, my real purpose is practical: to help people in their personal development and also to assist ministers within their specific pursuits. I seek not only to offer some spiritual and pastoral ideas which they might wish to apply to their own situations, but also to evoke and foster their own engagement in this kind of reflection. To this end I have tried to bring the discussion of each model into touch with some typical spiritual and pastoral problems and opportunities, with the help of several reflective questions at the end of each chapter.

It has not been easy to structure this volume, given the variety of models and the many possible linkages among them. But three of the essays are more foundational, and these I have clustered into Part I. Chapter 1 reflects on the theme of *energy* and *power*. All spiritual and pastoral situations, I believe, can be regarded from the standpoint of a single question: How do we disclose and liberate, for the sake of the Kingdom, the powerful energies present within all that is human? This first chapter is probably the most integrative of all, and can serve to keynote what I have to say. The second chapter reflects on Thoreau's symbol of the three chairs — standing for solitude, friendship, and society — and signalizes three basic dimensions of the human condition within which we employ our energies and utilize our power. The third chapter offers another "cut" into the human reality, the four Jungian functions of sensing and intuiting, thinking and feeling. Especially because Jung himself made use of the model of psychic energy, the link between this chapter and Chapter 1 is obvious. In addition, this essay argues that the four functions and their Gospel analogues may be viewed in their interpersonal and societal verifications as well as within the individual person; it thus establishes a link with Chapter 2.

Part II gathers three models whose development is primarily in the area of Christian spirituality, though I note also some pastoral implications. Each represents a fresh approach to some traditional model. Chapter 4 proposes a reversal of the familiar treatment of the theme of contemplation and action, and understands all genuine human action as both contemplative and responsive. On the way to this proposal I offer a theological description of prayer which emerged for me from the theology of grace of Karl Rahner. This theology provides a solid doctrinal base for the new action/contemplation model proposed by the

essay. Such a model, I try to show, can provide fresh energies for
the Christian's effort at integral growth.

Chapter 5 returns to a reflection of the mid-sixties on the
Spiritual Exercises of St. Ignatius, and argues that, from one
perspective, their unity and effectiveness may be conceived as
stemming from a certain rhythm of contemplation and decision.
It will be apparent how close this chapter is to the preceding one.
I also indicate that the Jungian categories of perceiving and
judging, dealt with in Chapter 3, broadly correspond to the alternation of the contemplative and the decisional in prayer.

Chapter 6 in its composition brought me back to a talk which
I gave again and again in the early seventies on the theme of
fidelity, which I saw as compounded of constancy and surprise.
What especially helped to make the presentations on this theme
effective with audiences was the fact that I used the rock and
the butterfly as symbols, respectively, of constancy and surprise; and the experience of waves at the seashore as expressive
of the integration of both constancy and surprise. I came to see
the traditional trinitarian model of God speaking the Word and
breathing forth the Spirit as the supreme paradigm of fidelity
conceived as constancy and surprise.

The final five chapters, constituting Part III, reflect how
much my journey has brought me beyond traditional spiritual
themes to social and cultural considerations. In Chapter 7, I try
to show how the traditional doctrines of creation and providence
are not a threat but rather a support to the human autonomy
prized by modernity. Chapter 8 echoes the discussions of the
late sixties and early seventies regarding development and liberation. My effort was and is to situate this distinction within a
traditional framework, the clash of Franciscan and Thomistic
schools on the relationship of creation, Incarnation, and redemption. The primary value of such unresolvable debates is to remind the disputants that they are in the presence of mystery
which no model of formulation can capture, and that every authentic word of faith carries the challenge to live the truth in
love.

For several years now the relationship of love and justice has intrigued me, and Chapter 9, building on two articles of the past decade, proposes a restatement of the insistence on integrating love and justice that I find very characteristic of the Roman Catholic tradition.

Chapter 10 explores a model which is most clearly not my own. It represents a large debt that I have to friends at the Center of Concern, who developed this framework for reflection for an important meeting of major superiors of religious in 1978.

Chapter 11, finally, deals with what is perhaps the most basic form of human energy, *culture*. During the past several years I have become convinced that spiritual and pastoral energies devoted to improving political and economic structures are doomed to sterility unless they attend to the cultural underpinnings of politics and economics. The Church's response to the problems of the global community must accordingly be focused as an evangelization of culture and cultures.

Since (as my room at home testifies) I am one of those people who finds it difficult to throw anything away or leave anything out, the writing of this book has brought the recurring temptation to toss in yet one more model, make just one more distinction, share still another insight. I hope I have resisted the temptation well enough to keep the main lines of the endeavor clear, and its content practically helpful. In an epilogue, however, I yield somewhat to my weakness by mentioning, for whatever value they may have to readers, several other models which have enriched me though the years. I conclude by identifying the area where my search for models now seems to be leading me.

Modelling

There is one other important task for this introduction, and that is the delineation with sufficient clarity of what I mean by the term *model*. This is not the place for an extensive treatment, historical or analytical, but something needs to be said. The physical and social sciences had been using the term and the

technique for a good while before theologians began explicitly to
do so. A little work of Ian Ramsey is commonly cited as articulating and spurring this movement in contemporary theology.[1] My
own introduction to this approach came with the work of John
McIntyre, *The Shape of Christology*.[2] Probably the most
tial book in disseminating this method was Avery Dulles' *Models of the Church*.[3]

In recent discussions of models in theology, the term is dealt
with in conjunction with several other terms: for example, symbol and image, metaphor and analogy, type and paradigm.
Without undertaking an extended discussion of such relationships, I understand "model" in the course of this book in the following way: A theological model is any term, image, concept,
name, or distinction, drawn from human experience and,
through the mediation of some insight, employed analogously to
search out and disclose some aspect of the mystery of salvation.

This broad description highlights four aspects of the modelling process in theology. First, modelling involves recourse to
some facet of human experience which has found expression in
words. Theology is inconceivable, of course, without human experience embodied in speech. In a world of parthenogenesis, for
example, God could not be spoken of as Father. Had humankind
never gone beyond hunting and agricultural modes of life, the
fullness of salvation could never have been named as the City of
God. This experiential reference of models is all too commonly
dulled by usage. It is of no small importance for our theologizing
that we bring to sharper awareness the links between language
and experience. This is one way in which creative insight is
evoked, and the sterility of traditionalism avoided.

Second, model involves a movement in faith from the reference point of articulated human experience to the mystery of
salvation. Because this is a movement into the depth of human
mystery, theologians have been at pains to distinguish modelling from anything like taking a snapshot or reading a computer
printout. Analogy is the principal traditional term employed to
signal this movement of faith from common experience and discourse to theological speech. Ian Ramsey's distinction between

descriptive and disclosive models — the latter alone being employed in theology — stems from a similar concern.

Third, it is at this critical juncture of the journey from common human experience to theological statement that the role of imagination and the act of insight is key. God as a wrestler, Jesus as a clown, the Church as a company of inebriates supporting one another around a lamppost — somewhere, in a flashing moment, some Christian saw that the mystery could be pointed to in yet another metaphor or analogy. Insight is the bridge from experience to the theological word.

The fourth important aspect of modelling has to do with its inherent purpose, which is both to express an understanding of religious truth already gained and to evoke further insight into and commitment to the mystery. The present book hopes to pursue especially this innovative goal of modelling, the opening up of fresh spiritual and pastoral vistas through the use of theological imagination.

The foregoing description may prompt some readers to ask, "Doesn't this mean that *all* theology is a process of modelling?" Yes, it does. One cannot theologize, professionally or at the grassroots, without speaking words, without saying something to someone. Theology is primarily a social behavior, in which the one theologizing says to some Christian community, "Could we not put it this way?" The chosen words reflect one's experience of life, and at the same time enunciate some aspect of the mystery of salvation with a view to grasping and living it more deeply. All theological discourse, then, involves models. What the authors referred to earlier have done is to make this characteristic of all theology a focus of method. A "models theology" is one which attends with special care to the words it uses, to their experiential basis, and to the occurrence of creative insight as springboard for every fresh leap of Christian understanding.

This leads to a final recommendation to readers. Because I believe strongly that the call to theologize comes with baptism and confirmation, and does not have to wait upon professional accreditation or canonical commission from the institutional

Church, I am also convinced that all of us have a responsibility
to develop our ability to speak the word of faith. The chapters of
this book will exhibit, narratively and reflectively, how one
Christian has been drawn to play with words in the house of the
Lord. The metaphor of play has been deliberately chosen, partly
in order to insist that theology is not to be reduced to the labors
of professionals. A theology which is always "dead serious" is inevitably a deadly theology. The game of theology, when it is well
played, refreshes and invigorates as any real game should. It is
a game that all of us can play. In the distinction of Dorothee
Soelle to which I shall return in the epilogue, my ambition here
is not to substitute for but rather to represent a common gift of
all the baptized — the power to celebrate in speech what God
has done, is doing, and will do, in Christ Jesus.

Two friends have been especially helpful in making suggestions for some of these chapters, and I wish to thank them: Sister Magdala Thompson, RSM, and Mrs. Arlene Gensler.

The Jerusalem Bible has been used for the most part in ren-
dering the translation of Holy Scripture.

1
Energy/Power

Though first in order here, the model of energy/power has engaged me deeply only for several years. Its emergence and the various linkages which it brought are typical, at least for me, of the way in which theological ideas take root and develop. As Chapter 3 will bring out, I had been working with Jungian personality types since about 1975. I remember being struck with Jung's language of "psychic energy," with which he modified Freud's "libido." As I began to make use of the concept of energy in talks on spirituality and on the vows of religious, it was a short and spontaneous step to recall Pierre Teilhard de Chardin, whose language of cosmic and Christic energy I had encountered in the 1950s. Soon there occurred the added delight of being brought back to an experience of my college years — about 1940 — when a chapter of Henry Adams, "The Virgin and the Dynamo," in his *Mont Saint Michel and Chartres*, contributed to my education as I recovered from tuberculosis at Saranac Lake. Keen excitement came from knowing that three major thinkers of quite diverse outlooks had been drawn to this metaphor. Innocent as I was of any sophisticated knowledge of the world of physics, the term took on for me a great deal of symbolic power.

What especially served to integrate some simple insights was the realization that the New Testament — particularly in the Pauline captivity letters, the Gospel portrayals of the ministry of Jesus, and the book of Revelation — was in effect an inspired commentary on energy and power, divine, human, and cosmic. Further enlightenment came from what a friend, Sister Mary Daniel Turner, was saying and writing about ecclesial and ecclesiastical power. Finally, within a few days of my return to

my native island of Manhattan in the summer of 1982, I benefited from talks given at the Catholic Theological Society of
America convention by John Coleman, Robert Bellah, and
others, on the theme of power. The highlight of that academic
meeting was skipping a few sessions in order to join the 750,000
people who had gathered in Central Park to say something
about the ways in which human power and energy ought and
ought not be used in our world. It was June 12, 1982.

Power: Modern Writers and New Testament

When Henry Adams stood at the Great Exposition in Chicago
in 1900 and contemplated the Dynamo, he reflected with melan-
choly on how the power of the Virgin Mary, which had energized
the medieval world, was a complete stranger in America. "The
highest energy ever known to man, the creator of four-fifths of
his noblest art exercising vastly more attraction over the human
mind than all the steam engines and dynamos can mind; and yet
this energy was unknown to the American mind."[1] Years later
his poignant "Prayer to the Virgin," in which a dark prayer to
the Dynamo was enclosed, similarly laid bare the brooding intensity of this effort to link medieval and modern embodiments
and concepts of energy and power.[2]

Even as Adams meditated in Chicago, Carl Jung was beginning the medical career which would lead him, especially after
his break with Freud, to enunciate a world view in which the notion of psychic energy was a central motif. Particularly in
exploring — personally, clinically, and theoretically — the immense energies which reside in the personal and cosmic uncon-
cious of every human being, Jung placed the spiritual question
in new terms: How can the near infinite resources of psychic
energy be disclosed and set free for the benefit of humankind?

A few decades later, a French Jesuit priest, out of his World
War I experience, was likewise being drawn to speak of life in
the language of energy. For Teilhard all energy in the universe
was psychic, and the concept of consciousness was to be extended beyond the human to all of creation. Like Adams and

Jung, though with considerably more optimism than either, Teilhard saw the universe as an immense and unfathomable energy system, on whose wise governance the future of humankind depended.

Of the three thinkers, it was Teilhard who stood most fully and unambiguously within the Christian tradition. When he sought confirmation of his vision in the Scriptures, it was to Paul, especially in Ephesians and Colossians, that he had recourse. My interest here is not to validate this recourse, but merely to show that in the Pauline corpus and elsewhere in the New Testament the mystery of salvation in Christ is prominently conceived through the model of energy and power.

If one recalls that in physics the ultimately indefinable notions of energy, power, work, and force, are closely linked, and then looks for such terms in Pauline usage, it becomes clear that a theological model employing such terms is well grounded. Greek terms like *ergon* and *ergazesthai*, *energeia* and *energein*, *exousia* and *dynamis*, and several others, flow abundantly in the New Testament books. Here are just a few examples: "God's power, working in us . . . " (Ephesians 3:20); " . . . how infinitely great is the power that he has exercised . . . the strength of his power in Christ . . . " (Ephesians 1:19-20); " . . . work for your salvation . . . it is God . . . who puts both the will and the action into you . . . " (Philippians 2:12-13); " . . . I struggle on, helped only by his power driving me irresistably . . . " (Colossians 1:29); " . . . The working of his power . . . " (Ephesians 3:7). It is unfortunate that our English translations rarely use the terms energy and energize, for these are in fact among the most frequent terms used by Paul to communicate the immense power and energy present in the world through the gift of the Spirit, as well as the energetic striving response which this divine initiative evokes in believers. Unfortunately, as Dietrich Bonhoeffer has noted, a quietistic misinterpretation of the Pauline insistence on God's gracious initiative has led many to miss what is obvious in Paul's own behavior even more than in his teaching, namely that we disciples are called to accept power and to use it by acting vigorously in response to God's call.[3] In one interpretation, at least, this is the paradox that Paul expresses in Philippians 2:12-13. It is not in spite of but because of God's working in us that we are to struggle for salvation for ourselves and others. God's gift in us is precisely the firm will to struggle and the victorious accomplishment of that struggle.

Paul did not merely talk about power and energy. He himself in his person and ministry was a living embodiment of the power of the risen Lord, working in a transformed history through the gift of the Spirit. The origins of this power are in the life and ministry of Jesus himself, which can be studied from the standpoint of this chapter. It is clear from all four gospels that Jesus was highly conscious of his own power, and aware that his mission involved a power struggle of cosmic proportions. He was sent to proclaim and institute the reign of God. The establishment of that reign involved conflict with the forces enslaving humankind. Jesus' total ministry, but especially his healing miracles, represented a vigorous assault on the evil empire. "If it is through the Spirit of God that I cast out devils, then know that the kingdom of God has overtaken you" (Matthew 12:28).

Even from a purely human point of view, the ministry of Jesus is manifestly an evocation, a liberation of the energies of those who came into contact with him. Wherever he went, hope and courage were born. When he touched people, they sprang up into life and action. The current phrase, "enabling leadership," finds a model in this healer whose typical word to those whom he had cured was *"Your* faith has made you whole." He was saying in effect: "You have power. You can do it. Cease wasting your resources by sin. You are capable of glorifying God." Truly power went out from him and healed many (Mark 6:19).

The gospels also disclose to us that this empowerment of his people was not without a price. It sometimes cost him groans of anguish (John 11:33, 38; Mark 7:34), and he was at times impeded by the resistance of unbelief (Matthew 13:58). Eventually the powers of darkness working through human agencies did him in. The mysterious law of the empowerment of the powerless, which we shall later describe, had to be exemplified in Jesus, the first of the *anawim*. The resurrection represents

God's central deed of power, the radical re-energizing of an impotent universe. The cross, inseparable from the resurrection, now participates in its power and energy. "And when I am lifted up from the earth, I shall draw all to myself" (John 12:32). Well did Christian art come to depict the Savior as *pantokrator* — the omnipotent one. It is a dangerous representation, of course, needing constantly to be counterpointed by the image of the Suffering Servant. But it has its necessary place. Within the basic paradox, we need to look at Jesus as source of radical power and transfigured energy.

A Theology of Power

Theological reflection on the theme of power and energy draws, as all modelling does, on a particular facet of human experience. Scientist-theologians like Teilhard have the advantage of a sharp and deep understanding of the rather abstract categories of physics. Non-scientists like myself can at best echo formal definitions of *energy* — the capacity to do work; *power* — the rate of doing work or the rate of energy flow; *work, force* and so on. Those who have read Teilhard's *Phenomenon of Man* know how this genius — poet and mystic as well as scientist — was able to translate his experience as a scientist into language intelligible for the general public. Such a path is not possible here.

Fortunately, there is an alternative. Our language of energy and power, whatever its relationship to the world of physics, more immediately reflects such common experiences as being tired or refreshed, lifting heavy objects, wrestling with another person, and so forth. We also transfer the terms derived from such physical experiences to our psychic, mental, and spiritual experiences. We speak of mental or emotional fatigue or exhaustion, psychic energies, and spiritual struggle. Some days — or most days — we may suffer from depression, and we also know the experience of ebullient well-being which leaves us ready to take on the world. For most of us, common or everyday experiences like these provide the reference points in our personal history for grasping the language of Scripture and theology when they speak of energy and power.

It is well, then, before summarizing some salient facets of a theology of power and energy, to tap into our personal experience. When in my history have I felt empowered and energetic, in work or relationships or interior life? When did depression or a sense of frustration drain me of desire and hope? The Gospel of the empowering Spirit will be truly good news for me to the degree to which I am in touch with my need for it, as well as with its correspondence with my deepest yearnings.

Here then are some basic affirmations regarding energy and power. First, the risen Christ, gifted by the Father with unlimited power, and a subject of immense energy, shares that gift with the rest of humankind through the gift of the Spirit. Since the resurrection, ascension, and Pentecost, the deepest reality of the world is the Spirit of God immanent in all its human and cosmic processes.

Second, the principal carrier of the power and energies of the divine Spirit is the human spirit enfleshed in world history. All the resources of individuals, groups, and societies are the vehicles of saving power, channels of divine energy. Our memories, imaginations, minds, feelings — all of our physical and psychic resources, as well as our interpersonal and societal processes of every kind — mediate God's power and energy to the world. From this standpoint, the universe is an inexhaustible energy system whose very soul is God, divine Spirit.

Third, the forces of evil, though definitively overcome through the death and resurrection of Christ, continue to exist and struggle with the power of God. Radical spiritual conflict is a basic law of life. The very same human resources which carry the energies of the Spirit are also carriers of dark and destructive forces. This is a way of saying that sin and grace, concupiscence and charity, coexist and struggle within persons, within their relationships, and in the forms of human society and culture.

Fourth, the message of the Cross and resurrection as it touches this struggle celebrates the wondrous paradox of powerlessness and power. Paul's eloquent formulation of this message to the Corinthians has profoundly shaped the awareness of Christians (1 Corinthians 1-2). Powerlessness as salutary, the foregoing of a certain kind of power as an act of wisdom — this is sound and crucial Christian language, despite its risks. Later I will suggest a way of dealing with those risks.

Fifth, the power struggle between Christ and Satan is cosmic in scope, and touches the whole of human and cosmic history. Still, there is one historical community, the Christian Church, which embodies in a unique way the divine energies which have entered the world at Pentecost. Among many possible ecclesial models, here the Church appears as a world-wide energy system, a kind of spiritual dynamo exercising a unique power for the benefit of humankind.

Power in Spiritual Growth

A power/energy model such as this can serve spiritual growth. Without disparagement of the value of other models — enlightenment, liberation, organic growth, transformation, and the like — this one has distinctive assets for the theory and practice of spirituality. The following observations will confirm and elaborate this.

First, spirituality may be understood as theory and practice touching the life of the human spirit in the world as shaped by the Spirit of God and in the face of evil spirits which still resist God. Such an understanding involves a focus on the presence of the Holy Spirit precisely as energizing and empowering us for the spiritual struggle. The former rite of confirmation contained the phrase, "Receive the Holy Spirit for *strength* . . . " (Accipe Spiritum Sanctum *ad robur* . . . ") — the strength of the oak. With baptism and confirmation, every Christian is fitted out with armor and weapons for struggle, exertion, contest. Life is intended by God to be intensely energetic, and to yield increasingly a share in the divine power. Such a spiritual model, though not the only one, has the advantage of counteracting any temptation to quietism, any attitude of "cheap grace," or any distortion of the Gospel ideal of childlikeness portrayed so attractively by St. Therese of Lisieux. God has provided each of us with immense resources of spiritual energy and has called us to share divine power. We are responsible and accountable for these gifts.

Second, the problematic of the spiritual quest then becomes: How am I to uncover and liberate the fullness of power/energy hidden in my humanity through the gift of God? Here is where an energy model can join with enlightenment and liberation models. The way of enlightenment described by both Christian and non-Christian spiritualities is thus conceived as progressive disclosure of the immense energies hidden within us. So many human resources are wasted because they are not permitted to come to the light. There are, for example, immense energies contained in forms of prayer which are totally unknown to most Christians. The play of fantasy, the deliberate emptying of consciousness in a centering exercise, the focusing of attention on a flower or a sound — such exercises can make us aware of how richly endowed we are. All too commonly Christians let such possibilities escape their notice and engage instead, sometimes in the guise of prayer, in compulsive or neurotic behaviors which merely react to this or that stimulus. Enlightenment, then, means that the growing Christian, helped often by a wise guide or supportive community, will learn gradually to come into touch with hidden energies.

Something similar may be said of the *liberation* of our power/energy. Traditional spirituality has used the term concupiscence to describe the unfree movements, in fear or desire, which make up most of the lives of the unconverted. Paul's poignant, "I find myself doing what I don't want to do, and not doing what I really want," is the classic expression of this enslaved condition (Romans 7:15). Human energies are wasted. Worse still, they are used destructively, to perpetuate the reign of enslavement. The fire and water of the Spirit bestowed for the nurturing of life become agents of death. From this perspective, the spiritual quest is a persevering effort to set our human energies free for creative faith, hope, and love.

Third, as one engages in this struggle for enlightenment and liberation, the mysterious law of the Cross is experienced. One learns through the hard lessons of life that power becomes perfect in weakness. No single lesson of Christian experience is more crucial than this, and I would say nothing to weaken its absolute necessity. But I have experienced in myself and others that Paul's language to the Corinthians can become a hiding place instead of a challenge. We may become unduly enamored of the language of powerlessness, weakness, littleness, precisely at a time when God is asking us to accept empowerment and to stretch all our resources in responding to the challenge of "costly grace."

In this regard I often recall a helpful distinction which I heard about fifteen years ago in a speech on liberation. Elaborating, I would distinguish between:

> *power*, the good gift bestowed in our *creation* according to God's image;
> *impotence*, characterizing the reality of *sin*, hence under no circumstances to be loved or desired;
> *powerlessness*, as the *ambivalent* and *provisional* condition of the person or group oppressed by sin yet clinging in hope to the promise of God;
> *empowerment*, the name for God's saving action on behalf of the powerless, an action freely ratified by them.

In this schema power remains a human good, and we ought not be ashamed to seek it. We are in fact made for power, and need to accept responsibility for its right use. Impotence is hateful to God, a sign and effect of Satan's destructive reign. Powerlessness is already an incipient empowerment, for it is the result of grace and contains the faith and trust that the faithful God will deliver those who cling energetically to him in hope. Empowerment is what God has promised and will provide. Such a language helps us to deal with the contrasting temptations of a self-sufficiency that is pelagian and a self-inadequacy that is quietistic.

Fourth, we need to attend to the relationship of spiritual energies with various other energies which mediate and affect their
exercise. All human behavior is multi-dimensional: our juices
flow, our glands secrete; the steady interaction of unconscious
and conscious psychic powers continues; thoughts and images
and feelings and perceptions interweave with great complexity.
The point of adverting to this mix of energies is to insist on something obvious but often neglected. Bodily and psychic health, an
alert and well informed mind, disciplined habits and a con-
gruent life style — while they are variables, not absolutes — affect our growth in significant ways. Without questioning God's
ability to transform our weakness into power, it remains true
that a sound spiritual regimen will consistently attend to these
other kinds of energies. Losing weight through a more careful
watch over one's diet, getting a better knowledge of one's personality through such helps as we will be describing in Chapter 3,
or moving from the suburbs to the inner city — or vice versa —
are examples of the kind of pragmatic decisions which are
needed if all our energies are to be on the side of the Spirit.

Power in Ministry

Just as the power/energy model can help us better understand
our personal effort to grow in holiness, it can also throw light on
our ministry in the Church. Here are some specific reflections
which may spark further insights in readers. The very meaning
of ministry may be better understood with the help of this
model. I am thinking of a metaphor that is more psychic and social than physical — the image is not that of a dynamo or nuclear
reactor but more like the psychosocial ferment that occurs when
persons and groups endowed with charism act creatively in social and cultural contexts. From this standpoint ministry appears as *contagion*. A small group of persons has become infected with the Gospel, and makes itself present to others within
a specific milieu — a parish, a campus center, a house of prayer.
What was said of Jesus — "power went forth from him and
healed all" (Luke 6:19) — is verified whenever Christian presence becomes ministerial.

Such a model can help a ministerial team understand itself and its mission. *The problematic of ministry* now becomes: How are we to identify, evaluate, evoke, and direct the various forms of human energy present in our particular human situation? This basic question contains many more questions. For example: What power/energy can be identified within each minister and within the ministry team as a whole? What talents and gifts in ourselves do we need to recognize, call forth, and harmonize? Similarly, what power/energy do we find in those to whom we have been sent? Where are the hidden or paralyzed forms of human power which the Spirit of God through our efforts wishes to disclose and set free? What, for example, is the unrealized potential of the residents of a local retirement home, not merely to be objects of our ministry but to be themselves agents of ministry? How can we so invest our energies in ministering to these senior citizens as to elicit their full and distinctive engagement in our common mission as a Christian community?

When we *evaluate* the various facets of ministry, how do they appear from the standpoint of energy and power? Do our Sunday celebrations enliven or deaden people's sense of their potential? Have we sufficiently attended to the power of music and song, play and leisure, in the liturgical and devotional and recreational life of our community? Are CCD classes merely fulfilling a pastoral responsibility to public school children, or are they scenes where, despite the immense pressures stemming from the prevailing youth culture of today, young people are put in touch with their true worth, their capacity to become good news for others.

Similarly, are we in touch with *societal despair*, that is, with the loss of psychic and spiritual energy and power coming from a largely repressed anticipation of nuclear disaster or ecological catastrophe?[4] This buried wound to human hope is more pervasive and more dangerous than the personal anxieties about specific evils that most of us carry around with us. Psychologists and psychiatrists have recently warned of the damaging impact on children and adolescents of the climate of fatalism generated by the arms race and by our worsening relationship to the

earthly environment. The Gospel of Jesus Christ has power to
bring hope to situations of despair, but the proclaimers of the
Gospel need to be sensitive to the culturally induced deafness
which deprives people of their human capacity to hear the Gospel when it is preached. Today, far more widely than we might
think, fatalism and depression sap the energies of people, old
and young, numb their sensibilities, and give the challenge of
evangelization an unprecedented intensity. True, the very desperateness of the situation represents an opportunity for ministry. But if the opportunity is to be seized, the ministers must be
in touch with the way in which such energies are flowing in the
world around them.

A power/energy model can also help ministry teams to reflect
on and exercise *leadership*. Whatever style of leadership may be
called for in a particular situation, its exercise always includes
the recognition, evocation, and shepherding of the total forces
present within a community. Not all leadership is official or
even formal. Where a community has come to such a degree of
maturity that participative and enabling modes of decision
making are effectively in place, the pluriform exercise of leadership can make the community a place where powerful energies
are being wisely directed to the spread of the Gospel. In any
case, those who have been designated to preside over the growth
of a community can fruitfully evaluate their own leadership by
scrutinizing what is happening to the power and energy present
within the community.

One important role of formal leadership is to pay attention —
and to direct the attention of others — to the *structures* which
the community has given itself. A power/energy model of ministry encourages the valuing of structures as vehicles for conserving and enhancing the energies of persons and groups within the
community. Without appropriate structures, personal and interpersonal energies are frustrated of their purpose or permitted to trickle away in ineffectiveness. On the other hand, structures that are procrustean beds or which are otherwise incongruous will repress the flow of personal and group energies and
will lead to sheer passivity, anomie, and acquiescence in medioc-

rity. Periodically, each ministry team needs to examine the existing structures which form the scaffolding of what it is trying to build — or better, which are the conduits and channels which carry the precious flowing energies of the community.

Finally, and most important of all, the theme of power/energy *becomes* the Gospel that is proclaimed. As Christianity is a song about freedom, about light, about beauty, about intimacy, about an endless series of symbols which carry our humanity, so is it a song about energy and power. At a juncture of history when the Gospel is being seen as a call to *justice*, recourse to an energy/power model can be enlightening. From this point of view, the radical injustice which afflicts our world today appears as a squandering and abuse of God-given energies. The primary energies in question are not the physical resources of our universe, however responsible we may be for these. Rather, the denouncing of injustice and announcing of justice which distinguishes today's evangelization need to be focused on the scandalous misuse and waste of *human* energies — physical, psychic, intellectual, moral, cultural, and especially spiritual. For example, in a factory making nuclear warheads, what cries out to God for vindication is not so much the fact that the gift of earthly resources is being used to fashion gods of hellish destructiveness. It is rather the fact that human beings, created in God's image and restored by Christ's death to that image, are using their personal talents and gifts, their capacity for teamwork, their loyalty, their dedication to truth, in the service of the enemy of humankind. That this takes place in large part without bad faith on the part of these unwitting captives renders the situation all the more tragic. To this example could be added countless others, such as the way in which Hollywood and Madison Avenue devour rich gifts of imagination and passion, for the entertainment mills which keep the public numb to the real challenges of life.

When we *evaluate* the various facets of ministry, how do they appear from the standpoint of energy and power? Do our Sunday celebrations enliven or deaden people's sense of their potential? Have we sufficiently attended to the power of music and song, play and leisure, in the liturgical and devotional and recreational life of our community? Are CCD classes merely fulfilling a pastoral responsibility to public school children, or are they scenes where, despite the immense pressures stemming from the prevailing youth culture of today, young people are put in touch with their true worth, their capacity of become good news for others.

Similarly,are we in touch with *societal despair*, that is, with the loss of psychic and spiritual energy and power coming from a largely repressed anticipation of nuclear disaster or ecological catastrophe?[4] This buried wound to human hope is more pervasive and more dangerous than the personal anxieties about specific evils that most of us carry around with us. Psychologists and psychiatrists have recently warned of the damaging impact on children and adolescents of the climate of fatalism generated by the arms race and by our worsening relationship to the earthly environment. The Gospel of Jesus Christ has power to bring hope to situations of despair; but the proclaimers of the Gospel need to be sensitive to the culturally induced deafness which deprives people of their human capacity to hear the Gospel when it is preached. Today, far more widely than we might think, fatalism and depression sap the energies of people, old and young, numb their sensibilities, and give the challenge of evangelization an unprecedented intensity. True, the very desperateness of the situation represents an opportunity for ministry. But if the opportunity is to be seized, the ministers must be in touch with the way in which such energies are flowing in the world around them.

A power/energy model can also help ministry teams to reflect on and exercise *leadership*. Whatever style of leadership may be called for in a particular situation, its exercise always includes the recognition, evocation, and shepherding of the total forces present within a community. Not all leadership is official or even formal. Where a community has come to such a degree of maturity that participative and enabling modes of decision making are effectively in place, the pluriform exercise of leadership can make the community a place where powerful energies are being wisely directed to the spread of the Gospel. In any case, those who have been designated to preside over the growth of a community can fruitfully evaluate their own leadership by scrutinizing what is happening to the power and energy present within the community.

One important role of formal leadership is to pay attention — and to direct the attention of others — to the *structures* which the community has given itself. A power/energy model of ministry encourages the valuing of structures as vehicles for conserving and enhancing the energies of persons and groups within the community. Without appropriate structures, personal and interpersonal energies are frustrated of their purpose or permitted to trickle away in ineffectiveness. On the other hand, structures that are procrustean beds or which are otherwise incongruous will repress the flow of personal and group energies and will lead to sheer passivity, anomie, and acquiescence in mediocrity. Periodically, each ministry team needs to examine the existing structures which form the scaffolding of what it is trying to build — or better, which are the conduits and channels which carry the precious flowing energies of the community.

Finally, and most important of all, the theme of power/energy *becomes* the Gospel that is proclaimed. As Christianity is a song about freedom, about light, about beauty, about intimacy, about an endless series of symbols which carry our humanity, so is it a song about energy and power. At a juncture of history when the Gospel is being seen as a call to *justice*, recourse to an energy/power model can be enlightening. From this point of view, the radical injustice which afflicts our world today appears as a squandering and abuse of God-given energies. The primary energies in question are not the physical resources of our universe, however responsible we may be for these. Rather, the denouncing of injustice and announcing of justice which distinguishes today's evangelization need to be focused on the scandalous misuse and and waste of *human* energies — physical, psychic, intellectual, moral, cultural, and especially spiritual. For example, in a factory making nuclear warheads, what cries out to God for vindication is not so much the fact that the gift of earthly resources is being used to fashion gods of hellish destructiveness. It is rather the fact that human beings, created in God's image and restored by Christ's death to that image, are using their personal talents and gifts, their capacity for teamwork, their loyalty, their dedication to truth, in the service of the enemy of humankind. That this takes place in large part without bad faith on the part of these unwitting captives renders the situation all the more tragic. To this example could be added countless others, such as the way in which Hollywood and Madison Avenue devour rich gifts of imagination and passion, for the entertainment mills which keep the public numb to the real challenges of life.

Clearly, then, energy/power offers us a first model which can both help us to grow personally in the life of the Spirit and to minister to people and to society. In most of the subsequent chapters we will attempt to indicate how the particular model under discussion may be viewed as a facet of this basic model which describes the very essence of the Christian life: the disclosure and setting free, for the work of the Kingdom, of the powerful energies given us by God. Incidentally, our description of this first model has manifested another model which is basic, expressed in the twin concepts of *awareness* and *freedom*, or *enlightenment/ liberation*. Every major spirituality, Christian or not, offers both a way of enlightenment and a way of liberation, deliverance from illusion and avoidance, on the one hand, and deliverance from enslaving concupiscence on the other. Similarly, all evangelization, in whatever form of ministry we practice, seeks both to enlighten and to free, so that the power of the Spirit, now deeply immanent in humankind and in the whole of creation, may progressively energize all that happens on this earth.

Questions for Reflection

1. How would I go about an inventory of the energies which form the basis of my discipleship and stewardship?

2. Where do I experience in my life the waste of human energies?
3. How would I describe this or that kind of human encounter from the standpoint of the positive and negative energies at work in the encounter?
4. What are my preferred ways of speaking about power and powerlessness?
5. If I minister to others, especially as part of a team effort, how would I describe, from a power/energy standpoint, the goal of such ministry? How would I evaluate the actual exercise of ministry? What barriers exist to effective ministry, and what strategies and models might serve to remove those barriers?

2
Solitude/Friendship/Society

In the fall of 1973, the Center of Concern, barely out of infancy, put together a publication linking Ignatian spirituality with the social concerns for whose promotion the Center had been founded in 1971. Thirteen Jesuits, representing the two facets of ministry being linked, met four times for intensive dialogue and work sessions. A fourteenth participant, Sister Margaret Brennan, IHM, helped to keep the project from being — rather typical for that time — a totally in-house Jesuit undertaking. With amazing economy and solidarity, we were able in just four one-day meetings over a period of six months to compose, revise, and criticize a set of essays which appeared in tabloid form in the fall of 1974 as *Soundings: A Task Force on Social Consciousness and Ignatian Spirituality*.

The Three Chairs

In our early discussions several participants spoke of the influential work of Peter Berger and Thomas Luckmann, *The Social Construction of Reality*. At some point in listening, a spark of intuition was struck in a few of us, which brought forth first a flickering, then a steady insight; and there was generated a model which Peter Henriot and I have used over and over for more than a decade. It perceives human reality to be constituted in three dimensions: intrapersonal, interpersonal, and societal or public. My own essay in *Soundings* picked up the then current jargon of "social sin," and made the new point that, to be faithful to the Christian vision, we must also speak of "societal *grace*." In subsequent years I have used this societal sin/societal grace model in a dozen different ways for analyzing and reflecting on spiritual and pastoral issues. For example, in 1975 I tried to illustrate in more detail how Ignatian spirituality needed to

18

take cognizance of the societal dimension of the human, particularly in some of the key meditations of the Spiritual Exercises.[1] In 1978 a project similar in process to the *Soundings* project, but now undertaken by Bill Callahan and the Quixote Center, found me applying the triad to prayer in solitude, group prayer, and liturgical prayer.[2] As late as 1983, when Peter Henriot and I, together with Alan McCoy, were asked to speak at the annual assembly of the Major Superiors of Men in Boston, we found ourselves structuring our presentations according to the same triad.[3]

It was Sister Jose Hobday who acquainted me with the symbolic language of Thoreau, expressing the same insight when he wrote:

"I had three chairs in my house; one for solitude, two for friendship, three for society."[4]

Sister Jose's talk at the Eucharistic Congress in Philadelphia in 1976 transformed the three chairs into three tables. She eloquently described how each of us needs to banquet at the table of solitude — in prayer apart; of friendship — in our communion with friends; and in society — when we make the hungers of the human family our own. I was much pleased around 1981 when a fellow Jesuit, Jim Stormes, chose to write the paper required to receive his Master's in Divinity degree from Weston College around the notion of societal grace. Also, a book by Francis Meehan a few years ago drew on the model as developed by Peter Henriot and me. If I had to choose among the models discussed in this book, this one would perhaps be my favorite, especially when it is crossed, as in the following reflections, with the Pauline model of creation/sin/redemption.

"Christian anthropology" is a phrase which has found its way into theology in the past few decades. Bearing different senses in different theologies, generally it carries the conviction that our knowledge of the divine is interdependent with our knowledge of the human. Some philosophical system or school, for example existentialism, neo-Thomism, or process thought, is usually drawn on to provide a specific model for the human. Thus traditional understandings of Christian faith are given a fresh enunciation and a new language.

The anthropological model of the human which I now set forth is more descriptive and practical than ontological or deeply analytical. It stems less from a particular philosophical point of view than from common observation of human beings. It owes something to the Berger-Luckmann construct, and more broadly to the insights into human reality which sociology and anthropology have yielded in the past century.

Both in secular and in ecclesiastical circles we have become accustomed to speaking of the individual in society, of the social character of personhood, etc. Such dyadic expressions convey a needed insight and caution — "No man is an island" — but seem to me to miss an important distinction. There is a qualitative difference between a person's relating to other persons in face-to-face encounters — in friendship, in family life, and in groups generally — and what happens when many persons, individually and in groups, create for themselves structures and institutions; or, more broadly, what I like to call "climates of life." The advantage of what I shall call here the Walden model — after Thoreau's three chairs — is that it makes explicit this important distinction, while at the same time insisting on the interweaving character of the relationships of persons, groups, and larger societies.

Let me first set forth, as simply as possible, this model as descriptive of our humanity. Then I will cross the model, so to speak, with the model of creation/sin/redemption. Finally, I will suggest some spiritual and pastoral areas where the model can be fruitfully employed, asking the reader to continue in this more practical kind of reflection.

Dimensions of Being

What does it mean to be human? The simple question provides an entry into reflection on the Walden model. Being human means first of all to be constituted as a self, a unique individual, endowed with personhood and interiority, with the capacity to say "I." I am myself, not you or anyone else. Being human entails a call to grow in my uniqueness, in the exercise of the virtually unlimited energies present within me by nature and grace. This first facet of my humanity finds exercise in *all* my behavior, but finds typical and symbolic expression in solitude, in solitary prayer, in lonely decision.

Being human has a second aspect, inseparable from the first. I can be myself, become myself, only as I live and grow with, from, through, and for other unique individuals. Human life is constitutively relational, interpersonal. Created in God's image, each of us reflects the trinitarian life which, as theologians since Augustine have taught, is constituted by the relationships of Father, Son, Spirit. This second facet of my humanity is exercised, like the first, in *all* that I do. Even in the most intense solitude my neighbor is hiddenly present. Still, certain types of behavior typify and symbolize this second dimension. In family, in friendship, in groups, teams, and communities of many different kinds, human beings are energized by this I/thou/we, face-to-face living out of the human call. As psychology tells us, and as our own experience testifies, these first two dimensions of being human are mutually interdependent. When there has been a serious family or community quarrel, it becomes difficult for individual members to go to bed in peace. When my personal prayer has gone well, I bring to encounters with friends and others a peace and joy which enrich relationships. Human energies are constantly being transformed from the intrapersonal to the interpersonal, and back again.

This interaction of solitude and friendship, however, is not all there is to being human. Moral theology, despite immense gains in recent decades, has largely limited itself to these two perspectives. Until recently, spiritual theology has even had difficulty integrating the love of neighbor into its conceptual framework. Fortunately we have come a long way in a short time to overcome such limitations. We owe it in large part to Karl Marx and to the great sociological pioneers of the last century or so that we now view the world also from a third perspective, which I have named societal. Christian theology and spirituality are now in the process of assimilating this anthropological insight. Theological methods, themes, and affirmations are all being affected by this major paradigm shift. The central thrust of what is called "political theology" as well as of liberation theology really has to do with the consistent appropriation of this new insight.

What writers like Berger and Luckmann have been analyzing in technical fashion may be more simply set forth as follows. When humans act as persons and interact within their personal relationships, this twofold flow of human energy generates a third current, composed of a wide variety of "climates of life." We all experience a broad spectrum of such humanly created climates, and we use several terms to designate one or another kind: language, symbol, system, structure, institution, society, culture. Such climates may be predominantly *physical*, for example the type of houses we build and the ways in which we adorn and furnish them; *psychological*, for example customs with respect to touching others in public and private, in secular and religious contexts (handshakes, hugs, kisses); *social*, like queuing up or not for buses; *political*, for example following a voting or informal consensus method of decision making at meetings; *economic*, for example diversifying crops with a view to a self-supportive domestic economy, as compared with concentrating on one or two crops in a predominantly export economy; *cultural*, for example rock concerts or Calvin Klein jeans; *religious*, such as vestments, incense, and other symbols within a liturgical celebration.

What is spiritually and pastorally significant about such climates of life is not just that we create them, consciously or not, as extensions of our personhood and communion, but that they in turn tend to enhance or disfigure God's image in us. No humanly created climate of life is purely neutral. The distinctive energy flow characteristic of this third aspect of being human coalesces with the energies of solitude and friendship in such fashion that life becomes either more or less human. All depends on the *quality* of energy flow.

Just as all that we do is both intrapersonal and interpersonal, so all that we do has a societal dimension, overt or hidden. Certain engagements in life, however, typify and symbolize our life as societal. The climates of our work and leisure, the ways in which we structure our sharing of meals, our habits with respect to travel or dress, can be either humanizing or dehumanizing in their effects. One of the popes (Pius XI, I believe), spoke of brute matter entering the factory and emerging ennobled by human toil, while the toilers often enter the same factory and emerge degraded by their toil. The work scene, whether factory or office or some other setting, can soil human beings in more than a physical sense, just because of the inhuman way in which it is structured. When this happens, the other two aspects of our life are affected. Our exercise of solitude as well as our communion with others is deeply dependent on the quality of our involvement in structures and institutions and other climates of life. It is likewise true, of course, that the positive energies which we bring from our solitude or our communion with others increase the likelihood that our efforts to make the climates of life more human will be successful, or at least will diminish the likelihood of our being deeply harmed by them. Reciprocal influence of each of the three circles of energy on each of the others is an important aspect of this model.

From Thoreau to Paul

It is at this point that what begins as a sociological model can take on the character of a theological model. An important and useful way to effect this transposition is to cross the Walden model — solitude, friendship, society — with a traditional theological model — creation, sin, redemption. I like to designate this last model as Pauline, because his version of the Adamic myth, and his depiction of Christ as the second or last Adam, is chiefly responsible for the major attention given this model in Christian history, particularly through the Augustinian tradition. This blending of the two triads can enable us to find a language through which our spiritual and pastoral practice may be viewed.

One may, first of all, look at solitude/friendship/society from the viewpoint of a theology of *creation*. What then comes into focus is the richness and the structure of our creation in God's image. From such a perspective we see the primordial human call as integrated from three qualitatively different components: a call to seek personal fulfillment, a call to ever deeper communion with others, and a call to build the human City in history as a prefigurement of the heavenly City of God. Each of these three aspects of God's image in us is a place where we are called to meet God. Because human life is one, energies flow from one sector to another and are transformed in the flowing. One might compare what happens here to the way in which different systems of the human organism — circulatory, respiratory, glandular, etc. — join to constitute the total life of the body; or to the way that within an industrial energy system the transformation of energy from kinetic to thermal to electrical is effected. What needs accenting is that in each of the three dimensions and in their interaction God is present, revealing and giving himself, and making the divine energies available for the exercise of our human energies. When one adds that this rich and complex human-divine energy system, composed of the resources of solitude/friendship/society, is situated upon the planet earth and within the total cosmos, interacting with cosmic forces of an infinite variety, there emerges a view of what it means to be human similar to that developed by Teilhard de Chardin. Readers familiar with his expansive view of humankind as situated within the "divine milieu" will know how to elaborate on the present model.

This creational view of the human, however, is a partial perspective. Still gazing at the human condition according to the Walden model, our grasp of it needs to take account of sin, especially of the radically sinful situation of humankind which has traditionally been called original sin. This second perspective invites us to gaze on the terrible waste and, worse, the destructiveness that invades all three areas of human energy when the dark power of sin lays hold of us.

This is not the place for a treatise on sin — its origin, nature, and effects. Our purpose will be better served by a couple of examples.

John is the unwanted fourth child of a father who, in coping with competitive pressures in business, succumbed to alcoholism, and a mother who kept unconsciously reacting against her own possessive mother. From early childhood he had to struggle with the neurotic feeling that he was of little value. In adolescence he sought a sense of self-worth within the drug culture of some high school companions. Not without gifts of intelligence and sociability, he graduated into membership and then leadership in the national drug traffic. Today he is an important figure in a criminal network which corrupts public officials, controls business and recreational enterprises, spreads addiction and other vices, and helps to influence the cultural life of millions on five continents.

Ellen, abandoned at age two by her battered and distraught mother, grew up in a public orphanage; and as a child she experienced both physical and sexual abuse. Her talents as entertainer provided her with escape and opportunity, and she became a Hollywood starlet. But her negative self-image and associated patterns of behavior inherited from childhood, an exploitative professional milieu, and successive betrayals by people whom she trusted brought her — after a brief and spectacular career — to suicide at the age of 36. On the way to this tragic personal end she was an important influence in changing sexual mores and in sparking the ambitions of countless teenage girls. She continues to live in popular culture and picks up new fans, through stories in magazines, reruns of her films, and an occasional TV documentary.

I grant that these are extreme examples, even stereotypes. Yet they do portray what takes place in the lives of all of us, in less spectacular form, to the degree that we live under the dominion of sin. The thing to be noted is the way in which negative, destructive energies flow back and forth among the three different dimensions — solitude/friendship/society. When self-contempt, denial, or any other form of psychological or spiritual illness afflicts an individual, such a person brings to relationships with others negative energies which make for disharmony, not communion. When people meet each other on the basis of what is chaotic and unfree within themselves, then with a certain inevitability destructive relationships will ensue. Furthermore, when patterns of dehumanizing relationships recur among large numbers of people, there are generated the societal climates, especially cultural ones, which are sinful and demonic, and which constitute that "world" which is the enemy of Christ and his Gospel. History witnesses over and over again that, given a certain coalescence of personal and interpersonal evil, it becomes an accepted thing within a particular culture to despise Jews or blacks, to exploit women, to manipulate the public, to do violence to the unborn and the newborn.

It is important to insist that the energy flow is from each of the three poles to each of the other poles. Sometimes people interested in spirituality speak as if all that has to be done to improve the world is to improve the quality of individuals; relationships and society will presumably fall into line behind personal reform and conversion. What is missed in such a view is that every effort at individual growth or conversion is conditioned by the quality of that individual's relationships and environments. It is no accident that the typical saint of the Church was in contact with other saints. Similarly, some of those who write about the transformation of structures and institutions as the key imperative of humankind today tend to neglect the interdependence of such transformation with the needed conversion of consciousness, and of human minds and hearts. For both spiritual and pastoral faithfulness it is essential that the analysis of sin and concupiscence in our world should, with a certain simultaneity, attend to how the kingdom of sin and death exercises its dark power precisely by dehumanizing the interaction of solitude, friendship and society.

There is, of course, a qualitative difference between the three kinds of energy, though each is truly human (or inhuman). This needs to be accented especially with regard to the difference between the interpersonal and the societal dimensions. The language of a law court, for example, should not be expected to have the qualities of warmth and intimacy characteristic of a meeting of friends. Sofas and armchairs are inappropriate furniture for the spaces where legal justice is meted out. Judges fulfill their responsibilities when they are fair, and even the compassion which they may show, for example to first offenders, is very different from the tender pity of a mother for her injured child. Granted that there is sometimes room for blurred borders between the interpersonal and the societal, life will be healthier for all if we appreciate that society is *not* just a family writ large.

The same insistence on viewing the human condition holistically is characteristic of the Christian view of grace and redemption, the third element in the Pauline model. In this connection I like to highlight Paul's statement which renders the heart of his joyful proclamation of the Good News: "Where sin has abounded, grace has abounded still more" (Romans 5:20). In present context this means that grace and redemption must be conceived triadically, that is, as working precisely in the interweaving of the energies of solitude/friendship/society. Again a few examples may be helpful.

Don is a prosperous broker as well as a husband and father of four children, now in their teens. Several years ago tensions at home and pressures at work led him to seek relief in alcohol — beginning with the extra cocktail before dinner and the nightcap for better sleeping, and leading to the three-Martini lunch, enjoyed with a few kindred spirits. Eventually his addiction brought him to the point of crisis at work and near disaster in his family life. Grace entered the picture in the form of a business associate who had herself walked the road of alcoholism, but then had found deliverance in Alcoholics Anonymous. Today Don gives thanks to God for the honesty and courage of one he counts as a true friend; two of his lunch hours and one evening back in the suburbs find him sharing his story at AA meetings. Peace has returned to his family.

Mary used to dread the bus ride to work in one of our major cities, most of all the jostling, competitive scene each morning and evening as people jammed their way onto the bus and scrambled for available seats. But one morning about a year ago, at her suburban bus depot, she had the angry courage to say in a loud voice, "My God, can't we act like human beings?" Her remarks shocked most of the jostlers, but next morning one of them said quietly to those who had come early, "Why don't we make a line?" For a week or so it was touch and go as to whether others would cooperate, but eventually with the help of some gentle humor, people got the point. The ride to the center city is pleasanter now, even for those who must stand. And Mary is hoping that the practice of lining up will begin to take hold also for the evening ride home.

A third story. One Sunday the new priest at St. Mary's talked about the dinner hour somewhat idealistically, as a sacred hour in the family. Bill and Maureen Kane looked at each other knowingly, each wondering how this young celibate would handle the restlessness and conflicting demands of three boisterous boys and their sensitive little sister. During the week, however, Maureen reflected a bit, and then proposed to Bill that they try a simple strategy. After the meal was well under way, each member would be expected to have one incident of the day to share with the others — without interruption. Bill listened to the proposal skeptically at first, but then, catching a certain sparkle in his wife's eye, responded, "It's worth trying." For more than a year in the life of this family, this formal time of sharing provided a modest structure within which each member of the family had the benefit of being listened to with interest and respect. It also helped these parents to keep in touch with what was going on inside their children, and provided them with an opportunity to praise and encourage each one. Years later the children would remember this little practice with affection and humor.

Look at each of these situations from the standpoint of God's grace. In each case it began in the heart of an individual person, was communicated to one or more other persons, and then became embodied in some societal climate — AA meetings, the practice of lining up for the bus, and a modest structuring of time within a family meal. Societal grace emerged from the grace of solitude and friendship, with a view to deepening the life of grace in individual and groups. What makes AA a societal grace is that it is not just converted individuals and the small communities they form across the country and in other countries, but the fact that it has become an institution in contemporary society which makes for a more human life. You can find AA in the Yellow Pages.

We are now in a position to blend the Walden model, being discussed in this chapter, with the energy/power model of the first chapter. What emerges is the necessity of conceiving the flow of sinful and graced energy as *always* involving the interplay of solitude/friendship/society. Under the surface of what might appear to be a purely individual deed of hatred or love, our sensitivity and analysis will disclose interpersonal and societal forces which promote life or death. A lone woman or man stands convicted of a most vicious murder, and spontaneously the anger of people surges toward vengeance. But let the story of this one human being be unfolded in detail, and we begin to appreciate that other persons and several social and cultural contexts had much to do with the tragic moment when personal energies were employed destructively. To say this is not to condone crime or to despair of individual conversion. Still, we are warned against interpreting and evaluating the behavior of individuals in isolation from their interpersonal associations and their societal contexts.

The same is true when there is question of behavior which might appear to be solely interpersonal or societal. What happens, for example, when a husband and wife make love is not exclusively personal relationship. The quality of the energy flow in each partner is feeding and being fed by the exchange of love. Also hiddenly present in this moment of deepest intimacy, helping it or hindering it, are the many societal and cultural contexts in which each of the partners is engaged day by day. Is the husband, for example, unconsciously swayed by a "macho" cultural stereotype of his manhood? Is the wife under the spell of subtle influences from soap operas or magazine advertising? The ride to work on the subway or commuter bus, the images experienced at the supermarket, and all the unnoticed languages and climates of the past day and week, condition the ability of even a very loving couple to make this a special moment of grace and sacrament.

It is the same for events that are overtly societal and cultural, such as a professional prizefight, a rock concert, a papal audience in St. Peter's. A certain anonymity and immersion in a mass of people characterize a flow of energy so powerful that it can induce ecstasy, frenzy, or violence on a massive scale. The moral and spiritual quality of what is happening is being secretly affected by the degree of personal presence (or absence) that each participant brings, as well as by the peaceful or troubled state of their most intimate relationships outside the mass scene in question. In turn, participation in such a mass cultural event will make a difference, sometimes profound, for the personal and interpersonal future of the participants. Whatever the specific impact, no one of us would have left a masterfully staged Nazi rally in Berlin or Nuremberg unchanged in our emotional or imaginative life or in the way in which we would relate to others in the future. The same needs to be said, though with less melodrama, of the many societal experiences which make up our daily lives.

Finding, Nurturing, and Releasing the Spirit

In summary, we have come in our reflection to a model of human and Christian life which sees the interplay of power and energy as exercised in the reciprocal influence of solitude, friendship, and society. Because ours is a Gospel perspective, what interests us most is the quality of the flow, that is, what is to be named as sin and what represents the gift of grace. Thus, from three areas or aspects of human experience worked on by the imagination, we have chosen and blended three ways of naming the human condition: energy/power; solitude/friendship/society; creation/sin/grace. We are now in a better position to say how, in a practical way, our spiritual and pastoral endeavors can be enlightened by such a combination of models.

One way of summing up the major fruit of this reflection is to echo the title of a little book of Jean Daniélou a few decades ago: prayer is a political problem. If spirituality has to do with the growth of awareness and freedom in the human spirit — both individual and communal — as that spirit engages the good and evil spirits which struggle for dominance in the world, then the insights of this chapter can profoundly influence our spiritual effort. Cognitively the spiritual quest consists of a process of *enlightenment.* Affectively it is appropriately described as *liberation.* We grow spiritually as we grow in awareness of and sensitivity to the competing forces in and around us, and in the freedom to choose how we will deal with these forces. The Walden model tells us that this process of enlightenment and liberation needs to include not only the discernment of spirits within our hearts but also what is happening in our interpersonal relationships and how we are being influenced by the surrounding culture. Because traditional spiritualities have lacked a language for this last area where spirits are to be discerned, there is a special need today to understand and emphasize it.

To make these observations more practical, we turn to what may be the key instrument of spiritual growth, the "consciousness examen" as it has come to be called. Building on the traditional examination of conscience, this exercise of prayer and reflection aims at heightening senstivity to and freedom towards various kinds of "spirits" or influences in daily life. St. Ignatius Loyola uses the terms "consolation" and "desolation" to designate, respectively, the experience of movement towards God and movement away from God as one engages in the exercise of faith. What the Walden model contributes to the discernment of spirits is the realization that, as William Barry has pointed out, consolation and desolation can have their origin not only within one's heart or in one's personal relationships but in the influence of one's cultural environment.[6] I may find myself, for example, lethargic and discouraged in my faith journey over a period of a few weeks. In personal prayer or with a spiritual director I ask why this is so. So far as I can see, the source is not in any change in my biochemistry or psychic life, nor do I find that I have been morally unfaithful. When I look at my relationships, my work, my religious duties, I find no "inordinate affections" which might account for my lack of devotion and zeal. If I keep listening to what the Spirit is saying I may find that some human environment whose air I have been breathing has been introducing attitudes, emotions, ideas, which subtly erode the power of the Gospel in my life. It may be a climate of ecclesiastical cynicism or secular despair which has been secretly contaminating the purity of my faith. Joanna Macy has written, for example, of the way in which the ominous threat of nuclear disaster has been generating in people a despair whose roots are societal.[7] She proposes that, as we have found ways to help people deal with their unacknowledged grief, so we need to use "despair work" in order to bring new hope to those whose lives have been blighted by the nuclear threat.

Another example comes from Janet and Robert Aldridge, parents of ten children, who heard and eventually heeded a radical call from God.[8] Robert was a nuclear engineer working at Lockheed on the Polaris, then on the Poseidon missile systems. This devout Roman Catholic couple, whose faith had been nourished by their involvement in the Christian Family Movement and in Cursillo, at first sought to avoid the message that God was sending them. But in the late 1960s their daughter Janie, concerned with the use of napalm in Vietnam, began to ask difficult questions in the family. Eventually this brave couple and their children came to know that they could have no peace with God and with themselves unless they acted on the call for Bob to disengage himself from making weapons of mass destruction. At the cost of a radical change in life style, and with a willingness to face an unknown future, this family discerned the violent spirits abroad in U.S. culture and found them contrary to the Spirit of Christ. Family energies, including Bob's professional expertise, which had formerly been squandered in homage to the arms race, today find expression in participation in the peace movement.

More recently, the widely told story of Justine Merritt and "The Ribbon" serves as another example of how the personal conscience of a solitary individual can lead to notable societal results. From the horrible moment in 1965 when she stood in Hiroshima and wept over what her country's political and military might had done to thousands of innocent humans, this one woman carried a memory which God's Spirit would never permit her to forget. Finally, during a retreat in 1982, she knew the course she was to take. Her imagination conjured up a simple yet brilliant strategy of enlisting thousands of people in sewing and assembling a ribbon which would be symbolically wrapped around the Pentagon. The themes displayed on the ribbon gave artistic expression to people's love for "what I cannot bear to think of as lost forever in a nuclear war." Thus, a tiny pebble of grace dropped into one solitary conscience made ever widening ripples of interpersonal and then societal love. On August 4, 1965, the dream came to fruition. What its societal expression in turn has done to form individual consciences and group concern is still an unfinished story.

For each of us the consciousness examen needs to be conceived in this enlarged fashion. We will always need to center it on what is happening within our own hearts under the impact of life's forces. But now we will be asking whether our awareness and our freedom are being energized or retarded by the confluence of forces coming from our solitude, our friendships, our engagement in society and culture. As a consequence our plan of life, our spiritual strategies, our specific resolutions, will no longer be limited to such areas as more regular prayer or kinder treatment of people. We will over a period of time make significant choices which reflect our growing awareness and freedom with respect to the various cultures in which we move each day. Diet, dress, travel, recreation and leisure, are some of the areas of life, which will feel the impact of this new consciousness and freedom. This is not a Manicheism which would denounce all participation in our society as inimical to the Gospel. But neither is it a bland cultural captivity blind to the presence of dehumanizing evil present in the very air we breathe — in TV sports, in soap operas, in the shopping malls of our nation. The Aldridges wrote of the choices which they found the grace to make:

34 — Playing in the Gospel

When the guarded gates of Lockheed clanged shut behind Bob for the last time, we started cutting expenses as an economic necessity. We ate less meat and experimented with new recipes that gave a balanced diet at less expense. Second-hand shops became our source of clothing. We discovered ways to reduce spending and approaches to pleasure without having to "buy" entertainment.[9]

Pastoral Ministry Implications

Obviously not all will be led by the Spirit in the same way or to the same degree of sacrifice. Just as obviously, no individual or small group can go it alone without help from the larger Church. Hence our reflection on the implementation of the Walden model moves from spirituality to pastoral ministry. We can only sample here the many questions which ministry teams will be prompted to ask about what they are doing and how they are doing it.

A basic starting point for such a reflection might be a contemplative gaze at the parish, the campus, the hospital, the school; a gaze which sees it as an energy system formed by the confluence of immense forces — interpersonal, intrapersonal, and societal. The children filing into the parochial school; the senior citizens assembled at the parish center or confined to one-room apartments; the spouses engaged in the twice daily ritual of the commuter railway station; and so forth. Each individual person and each set of relationships constitutes a concentration of human power and energy that is hidden or manifest, enslaved or free, and that works in favor of or against the coming of the Kingdom. As this complex dance goes on day after day, its quality is powerfully shaped by societal and cultural forces which, almost by definition, are hidden in the interstices of life. A major goal of ministry will be to bring to the light what is thus hidden.

Somehow, it seems to me, our ministers and ministry teams need to find space and time to attend to and to gaze on the scene of their ministry, and to see it as it is on multiple levels — demography, economics, politics, culture. They need also to be in touch with the way in which power and energy are flowing within and among persons under the influence of the total cultural milieu. Then they need to ask how this exercise of power, this flow of energy, is to be evaluated from the standpoint of the Gospel. Where is human energy being wasted because it is hidden? For example, what is the unrealized potential present in each aged and sick person within the parish, and in the encounters with them which other parishioners have or do not have? Where, too, are energies being squandered on what is trivial or even destructive? By and large, is Monday night football the great commercial and cultural influence that it is, because it is meeting the real needs of real men, or does it represent an escape, a moment of respite, for those whom neither the marketplace nor politics nor the Church is challenging towards more creative use of leisure?

Out of such questions, and out of the exercise of the Christian imagination of ministers, can come both dreams and plans for a kind of ministry which deals with the needs of persons and groups within the cultural contexts which affect all human behavior. Later, especially in discussing the "pastoral circle" in Chapter 10, we will have occasion to flesh out these remarks.

Let me conclude this part of my reflection with the observation that the effective minister or ministry team of today and tomorrow will need, together with understanding and compassion for persons, a feel for the importance of pastoral structures, especially at the level of language and symbol. Increasingly the ordained minister of the Church is being seen as called to community leadership. Where there is community, there is need for a common language, common structures, common climates of life, which express what the community is and wants to be, and which also enable the community to withstand the many hostile climates which menace efforts to live the Gospel today. The Walden model, joined with the perception of human and Christian life as a flow of energy and power, offers a reflective framework and tool which can assist both spiritual growth and pastoral planning.

Questions for Reflection
For personal spirituality:
1. Can I say that I have experienced in my own spiritual life both sinful and graced influences from the surrounding society and culture?
2. Do I have the habit of reflecting on such influences, in order to discern God's call? In this am I helped by the "consciousness examen"?
3. Do I have a plan of life which helps me to integrate solitude/ friendship/society?

For pastoral ministry:
1. What are some of the principal societal and cultural influences on the different groups to which we minister? Which climates could be named as sinful, and which as graced? What ambiguities do we discern in such climates?
2. How would we evaluate the degree of awareness and freedom with respect to such climates within our ministry team and within the community to which we minister?
3. How conciously do we structure our own ministry, and do we periodically evaluate those structures from the standpoint of the Gospel?
4. To what extent is the structure of our ministry *dyadic* (individual and society), and to what extent is it *triadic*, fostering the energies of *groups*?

3
Sensing/Intuiting/Thinking/ Feeling

Sister Magdala Thompson first introduced me to the Myers-Briggs Type Indicator Test. I had first met her when, as a Woodstock faculty member, I had gone over to the Sisters of Mercy community at Mount Saint Agnes College in Baltimore. In the late sixties she had gone to Michigan State for doctoral studies. There one of her professors was Harold Grant, who was imaginatively developing the implications of the work of Isabel Briggs Myers on personality types. Back at Mount Saint Agnes, Magdala shared with me her enthusiasm for this Jungian instrument of personal development. Under her direction I answered and interpreted the MBTI questionnaire, which disclosed, through my four-letter code (INFJ), that my favorite behavior was to dream up possibilities all by myself and, after that, to explore them with others in a feeling way. Little did I realize at the time that this new tool would provide so many opportunities for theologizing — as well as so much sheer fun — in the following decade and more.

A few years later, about 1972, George Wilson, a colleague at Woodstock (which by now had moved to New York City) and a fellow member of our small Jesuit community on Riverside Drive, began to do part time consulting work with Management Design, Inc. (MDI), a new Cincinnati firm which was beginning to develop Jungian models and instruments for helping groups and organizations. Some of the things that George said at that time, along with my subsequent association with MDI as a board member in the late 70s, brought the conviction that here was a model which, combined with the Walden model, would serve my efforts at theological analysis and reflection. Then, in

1975, Magdala and Harold and I gave the first of our retreat/ workshops based on the MBTI. By 1983 we had given over a dozen, developing our ideas and method as we went along. We had talked for several years of putting our approach into book form. Four months of a sabbatical spent with Magdala and Harold at Auburn, Alabama in the fall of 1981 enabled us to outline and then begin writing the book published by Paulist in 1983, *From Image to Likeness: A Jungian Path in the Gospel Journey.*

I have lost track of the number and variety of talks and essays in which this Jungian model has served to structure what I had to say.[1] For the most part I have confined myself to using the four functions — sensing and intuiting, thinking and feeling — as behavioral categories apt for correlation with Gospel themes and practices. In this endeavor Paul Tillich's term, "method of correlation," used by me in a sense quite different from his, has served to describe the movement from a behavioral model of the human reality to a distinctively Gospel one. Harold Grant's insight that the correlation be made through four Christian virtues has provided much of the energy of this endeavor, which still continues. This chapter will sample a few of the correlations which we have come to over the past decade or so.

Functional Types and Previous Models

Many readers of this book are familiar with Jungian typology, especially through the MBTI. There are also easily available sources for a more detailed presentation of this instrument of self-understanding.[2] A brief presentation here will serve as a review for some readers and as a needed introduction for others.[3]

Carl Jung's clinical experience acquainted him with the fact that while we all engage in common forms of behavior we also differ notably from one another in our behavioral preferences, and hence in the way in which we grow humanly. He used two generic terms, *perceiving* and *judging*, to designate the alternating rhythm, present in each person, of a) taking in reality, being shaped by it, and b) shaping reality, responding to it. Each of these two postures was specified, Jung postulated, in two contrasting *functions*. Perceiving (P) was specified as either *sensing* (S), the function through which, with the help of the five senses, we perceive reality in its particularity, concreteness, presentness; or as *intuiting* (N), the function through which, in dependence on the unconscious and with the help of imagination, we perceive reality in its wholeness, its essence, its future potential.

Judging (J) was also specified, in either *thinking* (T), the function through which we come to conclusions and make decisions on the basis of logic, truth, and right order; or in *feeling* (F), the function which prompts conclusions and decisions attuned to our subjective values and sensitive to the benefit or harm to persons which may result from our behavior.

All four of these functions, Jung affirmed, can be exercised by way of *extraversion* or *introversion*. He invented this now celebrated distinction to describe the flow of psychic energy in any given instance of behavior. In extraverted behavior the flow of energy is from the subject towards the object of perception or judgment. In introverted behavior, the flow of energy is in the opposite direction, from the object towards the subject. What makes the difference is not precisely whether the target of our perception or judgment is something outside ourselves or within ourselves, but which way the energy is flowing. Rather commonly, the impulse to share one's perception or judgment immediately with others or at least to give it bodily expression signals the presence of extraversion (E); a tendency to gather the perceiving or judging behavior and to deal with it off by oneself marks introversion (I).

Working independently of Jung, and on theoretical foundations previously explored by her mother, Isabel Briggs Myers developed an instrument which, on the basis of a preference questionnaire, indicated how the respondent likes to behave in given situations. The typology is based on four sets of polar opposites: extraversion/introversion; sensing/intuiting; thinking/feeling; judging/perceiving. In tabular form:

E — I
S — N
T — F
J — P

The four pairs of opposites in varying combinations yield six-teen types, each of which is identified through its code, e.g., ESTJ, ISFP, ENFJ. In the process of decoding, which we cannot describe in detail here, one arrives at the order of preference of the four *functions* (described as dominant, auxiliary, third, and inferior), as well as the *attitude* (introversion or extraversion) of the dominant function. Thus one person's most preferred be-havior will be extraverted feeling, another's introverted intuit-ing, and so forth. Also worth noting is that when the dominant function is a perceiving function (sensing or intuiting), the aux-iliary function will be one of the two judging functions (thinking or feeling); the third function will be the missing perceiving function opposite to the dominant function. A corresponding pattern will obtain where the dominant function is a judging function. This is one way in which Jung's view of "compensa-tion," or the balancing tendency of the psyche, is verified.

Extensive research and testing, especially with respect to the professions chosen by people of various types, enabled Isabel Myers to construct profiles of the sixteen types. These in turn have won for the MBTI extensive use in the fields of career gui-dance, personnel policy, and the dynamics of groups and organi-zations. The key psychological insight on which the MBTI capitalizes is that people's behavior, development, and relation-ships are strongly affected by their preferences in perceiving and judging, as well as by the extraverted or introverted charac-ter of the respective preferences. If one makes the assumption that persons are capable of enlightenment and growth through free exercise towards more human ways of living, this psychometric tool then becomes a vehicle of human develop-ment. Such is the conviction which has sparked enormous in-terest in the MBTI in recent years. Out of the work of these two American women has emerged the Association for Psychological

Types (APT), whose membership has reached 1500, and which has sponsored biennial conferences for discussing numerous aspects of the typology. One of the interest areas provided for in APT covers religious education, spiritual growth, prayer styles, missionary service and similar themes.

Such, in brief, is the typology which provides us with the model for the present chapter. Two remarks will serve to integrate this chapter with the two preceding ones. First, the notion of psychic energy was central for Jung, as I have already noted in Chapter 1. The problematic for the present chapter may, therefore, be stated thus: How can the resources of human energy contained in the four functions — sensing and intuiting, thinking and feeling — be described in Christian language, and how can these resources be disclosed and liberated in a spiritually and pastorally fruitful way?

Second, this Jungian model can helpfully be crossed with the Walden model. While both Jung and Isabel Briggs Myers centered on the individual person and on personal development, Jungian psychology is fully open to a holistic approach to the human, and specifically to an approach in terms of solitude, friendship, and society, as we have outlined in the preceding chapter. The preferred functions of each individual and the personal development which takes place on the basis of preferred behavior, profoundly affects what happens between persons, in friendship, marriage and family, and other group relationships. Marriage and family counseling, for example, often draws upon the MBTI to help spouses understand each other better. And so the interpersonal flow of human energy, described in the preceding chapter, can now be specified in terms of the four functions.

Similarly, the influential climates of life described in the preceding chapter can be regarded as differentiated according to the four functions. Cultures and subcultures, for example, tend to be predominantly sensate or intuiting, thinking or feeling, and characteristically combine a perceiving and a judging preference. A laboratory for practical research will prize sensing and thinking. The early stages of rehearsal for a Broadway mus-

ical, on the other hand, will more likely have an atmosphere that
is imaginative and innovative (N), and also rich in spontaneous
emotion (F). Or, in a large advertising firm, one might pass from
the room where ideas and designs are being generated to the
room where the firm's finances are managed, and experience a
radical difference in decor, dress, public mood, and whatever
else goes to make up the respective climates. Thus societal energies lend themselves to being identified with the help of the Jungian typology.

Analysis of Spiritual Movements

Keeping present to this image of human energies flowing
within, between, and around persons, we now ask how the Jungian model of the four functions can further deepen our grasp of
human reality. We begin with two generic designations of behavior, perceiving and judging. These terms can be taken to describe the rhythm of *receptivity* and *response* which Christian
tradition has dealt with in terms of *contemplation* and *action*.
To be contemplative, from this standpoint, is to be receptive to
the impact of life, open to God's self-gift as it is mediated
through every facet of the creation. To be active is to respond to
God's self-gift in deeds of love for God and neighbor. In the next
chapter we will explore further this correlation of action/con-
templation with the Jungian judging/perceiving rhythm of behavior.

Similarly, the Jungian division of perceiving into sensing and
intuiting calls our attention to what we all experience, namely,
the mediation of receptivity to the divine through receptivity to
the human (the traditional *pati divina* mediated through *pati
humana*). It happens sometimes in a focused, attentive, sensate
way; and sometimes in the dreaming, symbolic play of imagination or in the imageless gazing towards the Beyond.

In the same way the responsive phase of behavior, which Jung
terms judging, is expressed in two quite opposite modes — feeling and thinking. Whatever our preferences, some of our judgments and decisions are made on the basis of "reasons of the
heart," with sensitivity to the benefit or hurt which may come to

others; while other judgments and decisions tend to be cool and detached responses to what the objective situation requires.

The point immediately to be made is that a healthy Christian life, for individual, group, or organization, is one in which there is *freedom* to exercise whichever of the four functions corresponds to the needs of the situation, under the influence of the Spirit of God drawing one toward the appropriate behavior. Our behavior is Gospel behavior to the degree to which the receptive and the responsive, the contemplative and the active, flow back and forth in us without hindrance from inner concupiscence, the smiles or frowns of other people, and the seductive or hostile constraints of "the world."

It is possible therefore to take such traditional terms as purity of heart, detachment, indifference, which describe a basic disposition for growth as Christians, and to give them concrete form in the language of the functions. There is a time for everything — for paying attention in a focused way (sensing); for gazing dreamily at what might be (intuiting); for cherishing the intimacies and values which nurture us (feeling); for logical pondering of what is to be thought, said, or done (thinking). A sound asceticism will seek to develop by practice and discipleship an ever growing awareness of how these resources work within us, an ever growing freedom to draw upon each of them when appropriate, and an ever growing integration of these four facets of our personality. Freedom to do what one really wants to do and, as condition for such freedom, awareness of what one is really doing and really wants to do, constitute the key to Christian development. Human energies are wasted when they are not sufficiently brought to consciousness, and they are used destructively to the degree that we are not really free to direct them. When the rhythm of receptivity and response is brought under the sway of the Spirit of truth and freedom, then the life more abundant grows in solitude, in friendship, and in society.

One further observation on the functions will help to locate them from the standpoint of our situation in time. Students of Jungian psychology have noted that the sensing function tends

to be most at ease in the present; the intuiting function, our faculty of the possible, has the future as its home; and the feeling
function, which draws on the values inherent in our various her-
itages in order to make value judgments, makes the past a
source of energy. As for the thinking function, its role of providing order and structure correlates it with all three — past, present, and future.

When we put this time perspective on the functions together
with what we have said about freedom, then Christian "indifference" can be imaged in yet another fashion, as freedom within
time for the sake of eternity.

How can the insights into behavior contained in the four functions be made available for personal growth? I will respond to
this question in three ways, touching 1) forms of prayer; 2) the
practice of virtue; 3) dealing with crises in the course of life.

Types of Prayer

Prayer may and should employ all four modes of behavior. We
relate to God with no other resources than those which we draw
on for relating to human beings, to our work, to leisure, to the
daily round of life, to society. Hence, it is possible to designate
four generic types of prayer, according to which one or other of
the functions is engaged. Thus, prayer may be contemplative in
either a sensing or intuiting way. I can, on the one hand, practice
body awareness, or listen to sounds, or quietly look at the taber-
nacle or at faces of people on the street, or let the words of the
rosary flow from my lips. Such is sensing prayer. It is simple,
focused on the present, attentive to God through attentiveness
to some concrete mediation of God. On the other hand I can be
equally contemplative by letting my imagination engage in the
play of fantasy or daydream, as in the free flowing contemplation of the mysteries of the life of Jesus in the Spiritual Exercises of St. Ignatius. Or I may, as both Ignatius and Teresa of
Avila did, dream of myself performing great deeds of love for the
sake of Christ. A focused attentiveness or an unfocused and
vague expectation, the activity of the senses or the play of imag-

ination — both of these offer a broad variety of forms of contemplative prayer which can energize us for the struggle.

During a workshop sponsored by our St. Francis Xavier parish community in the fall of 1985, I led about fifty people in an interesting exercise of "Contemplation in the City." After disposing ourselves in the Mary chapel, each of us took a solitary walk in downtown Manhattan, invited either to *attend* to people, buildings, streets, sounds, or just to *gaze* in a general way at what we encountered. Some went to a farmers' market at Union Square, others to Washington Square Park, the heart of Greenwich Village, while still others worked their way along the predominantly Hispanic shopping district on 14th Street. For most it was a nurturing or exhilarating or peaceful new way of relating to our city, which so often terrifies or exasperates people. I encouraged the walkers to stay as much as possible in a contemplative posture, with no need to find rational messages or make value judgments about what they saw or heard. I offer this little example to point to the variety of ways in which people, in city or suburbs or small town or rural setting, can be encouraged to meet God in all things.

Prayer may also draw upon either or both of the judging functions in responding to life and to God. Prayer through the feeling function, for example, can take place when I gratefully recall persons, experiences, signal graces, of my earlier years; or when I lovingly breathe forth aspirations or praise God in song. The thinking function, often disparaged by people who, in their earlier education to prayer, had been oppressed by too cognitive approaches, is exercised in forms of prayer that soberly reflect on truth, order, meaning — or their absence — in my life. The traditional examination of conscience, or the weighing of life's priorities with the help of the Principle and Foundation of St. Ignatius, are instances of the thinking function at work in prayer. If our "Contemplation in the City" exercise had chosen to include judging modes of prayer, there might have been an exercise of gratefully cherishing "the Big Apple" as a city of rich gifts — ethnicity, culture, throbbing vitality, and myriad forms of compassion. Or there might have been an exercise of coming

to formulate some faith convictions about how we want to live in
the City as disciples of Christ.

What matters most is not which of the four functions happens
to be exercised at any given time in prayer — and usually each
function makes its way into most prayer periods — but rather
whether I am letting the Spirit draw me to those forms which
most energize and console me as I journey towards God.

Virtues

The *practice of virtue* can be aided by a correlation with the
Jungian functions. Basically, this is a game which anyone can
play. It has no probative value. Like other forms of play, its role
is to invigorate, amuse, energize. The criterion for the appropriateness of particular correlations is more aesthetic than rational — a certain congruity or fit between the terms associated
with each other. Over a period of years we have worked out a
few correlations, including the one which follows. I would not be
willing to die for it.

Sensing corresponds to the virtue of *simplicity*. To be matter
of fact, down to earth, to take one step at a time, to do what you
are doing — all these signal simplicity. The eyes of the servant
are on the hands of the Lord (Psalm 123:2); the soul is stilled
and quieted like a weaned child on its mother's lap (Psalm
131:2). There is no anxiety about what tomorrow will bring —
let tomorrow take care of its own anxiety (Matthew 6:34) — and
no extravagant expectations of what tomorrow may bring.

Intuiting corresponds to *hope*. Hope is the virtue which is
called into play when the message from present reality is grim
or dull. Hope is not optimism. It finds its support not in a rational analysis of the facts, but most typically in the face of what
the facts seem to portend. If simplicity is a feet-firmly-planted-
on-the-ground posture, hope is always leaping into the air without assurance that there is a place to land. Through imagination
hope creates out of a desperate situation the stuff of which
dreams are made.

Feeling correlates with *joy*, or more precisely with the joy of gratitude — *grateful joy*. The feeling function loves to remember past deeds of intimacy with loved ones. Like hope, gratitude knows how to break out of an oppressive present; unlike hope, which searches for the needed energy in the not-yet, gratitude finds that energy in the has-been. "Again the heart with rapture swells to greet the holy night . . . " As the story is told yet one more time, thanksgiving (eucharist) makes the primordial mystery happen again in the now and here.

The energies which flow from gratitude are often combined with those from a companion virtue, *compunction* or contrition. The past contains not only God's goodness but our reluctance to respond to it, our lack of gratitude, trust, and generosity. Sorrow really does build a bridge, over which we may confidently walk into the future because the past no longer burdens us.

Finally, *thinking* correlates with *justice*, the virtue which orders life according to some principle, norm, or rule. Every person, group, reality, has its just due. The thinking function operates whenever we seek to establish order in our life. We may, at least in a broad sense, exercise justice toward ourselves. It is unfair, for example, to our physiological and psychic life, to deprive ourselves habitually of needed sleep, or allow ourselves to become overly dependent on drugs or alcohol. Anyone who is serious about spiritual growth will establish some regimen or discipline which provides order and balance for daily living. St. Ignatius Loyola made a great deal of the need for order and the baneful effects of disorder. He stated the purpose of his Spiritual Exercises as consisting in "the conquest of self and the regulation of one's life in such a way that no decision is made under the influence of any inordinate attachment" (n. 21).

More properly, justice is an interpersonal and societal virtue. It facilitates right order among friends, relatives, colleagues, and within the family and other kinds of groups. When we come to deal with love and justice in Chapter 9, we will see that justice is not an alternative to love but rather an exigency of love, even a dimension of love. Justice does not cease or diminish as love grows. Intimacy and fairness support each other.

Justice is also, perhaps primarily, a societal virtue; that is, it facilitates public order. In our day the need for a spirituality of justice has been strongly affirmed by many. The insights of the preceding chapter enable us to appreciate that justice and injustice characterize societies as well as individuals and groups within society. Law is the most familiar expression of societal justice, but there are other forms as well. When we correlate the thinking function with justice from the standpoint of spirituality, it means that we need to regard not only whether we are just or unjust to ourselves and to other persons, but also whether we, perhaps unwittingly, participate in and help to perpetuate structures and institutions which oppress people and spawn moral disorder in the world. More positively, a spirituality of justice requires that we build into our lives concrete measures for sharing in the struggle to establish a world order which, in the language of Pope John XXIII, is " . . . an order founded on truth, built according to justice, vivified and integrated by charity, and put into practice in freedom."[4]

In such a spirituality it no longer suffices to give alms to the poor; we must also ask whether our invested funds are being used to promote justice or perpetuate injustice, whether, for example, we are patronizing the products of companies which exploit their employees or the poor of the third world. For such critical judgments regarding justice and injustice, our thinking function is the special gift bestowed by God.

Life Stages

A third relevant facet of the MBTI model has to do with the growth of individuals through successive stages of life. The constructs of Erikson, Kohlberg, Fowler, Levenson, Sheehy, Gilligan, and others offer conceptual frameworks for describing growth in our relationships with humans and with God. A distintive approach to human development based on the Jungian typology has been suggested by Harold Grant. As his hypothesis has been described elsewhere, only its bare outline and basic application will be delineated here.[5]

It is common to describe the order of *preference* which obtains with respect to the four functions. Intuiting, for example, happens to be my dominant function, and feeling is its auxiliary. The third preference will always be the opposite of the auxiliary (in my case it is thinking). The least preferred or "inferior" function will be the opposite of the dominant function (for me it is sensing). It is also common to describe an alternation between introversion and extraversion in the exercise of the functions. Since I prefer to exercise my dominant intuitive function introvertedly, I choose to use my auxiliary feeling function extravertedly.

What Harold Grant has done has been to move descriptively from an order of preference to an order of chronological development. In the example given, I would in childhood (6 to 12) have favored the exercise of introverted intuition. At 12 I would have switched into the extraverted cultivation of my feeling function. Early adulthood (20 to 35) would have been a time for developing introverted thinking, and from 35 to 50 my inferior function, extraverted sensing, would have heard the call to emerge into a fuller consciousness.

For myself, at least, the model fits my actual development. As a child in parochial school I often had to be summoned by the rest of the family from my inner dreaminess. My high school years found me really enjoying the extraverted feeling behavior of a scholastic debater, usually on topics which tapped deeply into human values. My early years as a Jesuit was a time when I found excitement in discovering and creating philosophical and theological models for expressing life's meaning. I was, in fact, at the beginning of this third period of development when the Principle and Foundation of the Spiritual Exercises, a short piece of abstract logic which Ignatius put at the beginning of the retreat experience, served as principal paradigm for the conversion which I then underwent. And in my later adult life I have experienced both my limited proficiency in sensing behavior as well as a real attraction towards developing my ability to pay attention to and live in the present. The principal discipline of my life for almost a decade now has been to develop by practice

and by following good example my neglected potential for finding God in the prosaic occurrences of daily life.

What I would emphasize here is that there are not only sea-
sons of a person's life but important turning points, often
marked by crisis and insecurity, and always full of opportunity.
This is true especially at the so called midlife crisis. Having
played the game of life from strength, as we are called to do, now
we hear a call to make room for weakness, powerlessness,
foolishness. If the inferior function — the beggar and the fool
whom I have repressed in the first half of life — is to emerge into
consciousness, then I need to let go of my inordinate attachment
to the exercise of the dominant function, with which I have over-
identified through the years.

What is intriguing about this developmental model is its congruity with the paschal mystery. Life must be lost if it is to be
found. The mighty must be dethroned and the lowly exalted if
the kingdom is to come within my personhood. The journey into
the dark night must be risked. The seed must die if it is to be
fruitful. All of the traditional metaphors and images used to describe the paschal mystery here receive a plausible developmental interpretation.

Limits of Types Analysis

Like all models, this one has its limits. We confront the midlife
crisis not on the basis of abstract typology, but on the basis of
the totality of our personhood and our history. Two things are
important, therefore, for people trying to use this model. The
first is that, if the shoe doesn't fit, don't wear it; you could do
damage to your feet. It happens to fit me and a good number of
other people. But you may be different, at least as regards the
difficulty of sorting out the influences which have shaped your
behavior.

The second point has to do with the variety of such influences.
Those enamored of the MBTI as an instrument of self-knowledge can be tempted to find in their personality type the exclusive source of all their preferences. They can forget the impor-

tance of environment for human growth. Hence the MBTI needs to be enlarged with the help of some nature-nurture model of human behavior. A relatively simple model here would consist of 1) personality type; 2) personal history; 3) the influence of culture.

For example, suppose I am working at the continuing healing and development of my feeling function. First I take as my hypothesis that, as my auxiliary function, extraverted feeling had as its special period for development the years of adolescence. Then I look at my personal history, to see what were the factors which impinged favorably or adversely on growth in feeling during those crucial years. I consider the fact that my mother was no longer a support for me, since she had died when I was nine. I also look at the social environment. Excessive shyness kept me as an adolescent from those romantic relationships which can activate the potential for intimacy. A compensating factor, which I have already mentioned, was my involvement in debating and public speaking. I would add also the influence of the camaraderie connected with neighborhood and school athletics. As I seek to retrieve my "personal salvation history," I will look for the way in which the inner drive to develop my feeling side was helped or impeded by such factors in my story.

But I will also try to put that personal story in a cultural setting. I was an adolescent in the thirties, not the seventies or eighties. I was a city boy, not a farm lad. My ethnic background was Irish, not Italian or Polish. I lived within the "ghetto" of U.S. Roman Catholic culture three decades prior to Vatican II. The prevailing images, symbols, mindsets, assumptions, customs, styles, and so forth, of the various subcultures which made up my total cultural ambience had much to say about how much and how well my feeling function was developed during adolescence. I can engage, if I wish, in the same exercise with respect to the other functions, regarded in the period designated by psychic nature for their emergence.

For this endeavor to retrieve one's personal history, a reflective framework proposed by Magdala Thompson, borrowing from Mortimer Adler, is quite helpful. In each stage of development I will look for three kinds of impact from the personal and cultural environment: 1) constraints; 2) pressures; 3) enabling opportunities. The first two of these tend to impede growth either by repressing inner drives or by pushing one beyond present capabilities. The third is constituted by environment, especially the loving and respectful behavior and attitudes of significant persons, which invites a free response to life's challenges. A child naturally given to emotional expression can be constrained by parents who frown upon strong manifestations of feeling in themselves and others. A son or daughter with little or no musical interest can be pressured into fulfilling the often frustrated dream of parents. And a child whose parents alertly watch for signals of readiness for this or that kind of growth, and then provide opportunities while leaving the choice of interest or career to the young person, is blest indeed.

In summary, then, the MBTI, in a developmental interpretation which also incorporates reflection on personal history and on the influence of culture, can assist continuing development in later life.

Contemplative Ministry

The basic model of this chapter also admits of utilization of a more pastoral kind. Let me elaborate three applications. The first concerns the importance of attending to the contemplative dimension of ministry. Here the reference is to both of the perceiving functions, sensing and intuiting, which we have seen to be correlative with the posture of contemplation. In sensing, this receptivity has a focused character; in intuiting, it is unfocused.

What does this have to say to pastoral ministers? Well, it seems to me that our models for ministers have been too exclusively tilted in the direction of doing things for others, fulfilling their needs; and not sufficiently attentive to the aspect of servanthood which consists in paying attention. All too often ministry has a substitutional character, and the unacknowledged need of the minister to be a benefactor of the ones served is satisfied at the expense of the latter. This is true especially of the need of people to be received, heard, listened to, and accepted as capable of directing their own lives and contributing to the happiness of others. Especially in dealing with the poor, doing *for* can unwittingly lead to doing *in* the ones we profess to serve.

In our world today there is a crying need for contemplative ministers, for people whose listening to God spills over into listening to the human beings through whom God comes to us. The whole field of psychotherapy and psychological counseling illustrates the power which ministers skilled in paying attention can exercise while appearing to say and do little or nothing. There are other pastoral contexts in which ministers can serve by just listening or gazing. To be willing to listen to complaints without defensiveness or recourse to facile solutions, to observe silently how people are behaving in various contexts (for example, watching their body language during a homily or meeting), or just to stand silently with them after greeting them, waiting invitingly for them to say what is on their mind — these are only a few of the many ways in which the eyes and ears of the minister can invite, from those served, an influx of spiritual energy into pastoral situations.

Back in the 1930s, for example, Sister Petronella, a Sister of Charity in our parish of St. John the Evangelist in Manhattan, asked her former pupil, Anthony Mestice, a high school student, whether he had ever thought about becoming a priest. He had not, but now he did, because someone who looked at him with love and hope communicated to him energy for dreaming. Almost four decades later, Sister Petronella helped to bring up the offertory gifts at the ordination Mass of Bishop Anthony Mestice in St. Patrick's Cathedral. Just asking a question — a truly contemplative act — can be a most powerful form of pastoral ministry.

It is interesting to study the ministry of Jesus for the pastoral questions he put to people, for example to his disciples at Caesarea Philippi (Matthew 16:13, 15); or the way in which he sometimes answered a question with a question of his own, as

with the coin of tribute (Matthew 22:20) or with the lawyer who
asked him what was the greatest commandment (Luke 10:26).
With full consistency Jesus noticed people, paid attention to
them, and only then proceeded to meet their needs in a way that
invited them to attend to their deeper needs. He also gazed on
people like Zachaeus or the woman taken in adultery, in a way
which generated in them hope that they could be better than
they presently were.

Quality of Ministry

A second way in which an understanding of the four functions
can be helpful in ministry has to do with the evaluation and im-
provement of specific forms of ministry. Here my suggestion is
that the four functions, together with the attitudes of introversion and extraversion, provide a holistic model for measuring
the quality of our ministerial performance. Gordon Lawrence
has show how this is true for the profession of teaching.[6] Those
who are teaching only from their preferred side will reach only
the corresponding side of their students. A teacher of Shakes-
peare, for example, who concentrates exclusively on the details
or the structure of plays — aspects which call forth the sensing
and thinking functions — without attending to imagery, fantasy, or emotional tone — aspects which call forth intuiting and
feeling, will be banalizing the great bard and cheating their students. By the same token, such a teacher will succeed in reaching certain students — the ones naturally drawn to detail and
structure — but not others — the ones who are bored by such
study but who would become excited if their symbolic imagination or warmth of emotion were engaged by the teacher's style.
Similarly, a pedagogy which provides no situations for learning
through lively interaction of students with the teacher and with
one another would be slanted towards introverted types. The opposite would be true of a pedagogy which did not invite students
to take the play into themselves for pondering.

One of the values of Lawrence's challenging book is that it
helps the conscientious teacher to evaluate the wholeness of the
pedagogical method and style being followed. A similar book,

based on Jungian typology, might be written for each of several
aspects of pastoral ministry. Closest would be the class in religious education or catechetics. Homilies might also be looked at
from the standpoint of the four functions in their introverted
and extraverted exercise. We might say, for example, that a
sound homily — whatever its accent — should have something
in it for sensing and intuiting, thinking and feeling. It is true
that in white congregations, the homily finds one person speaking and everyone else listening (generally in black churches the
congregation has a more active and vocal role). But a skillful
homily will have something for sensibility, for rationality, for affectivity, and (to coin a term) for imaginability. Listeners should
feel invited by the flow of the preacher's language to be, alterna-
tively, either attentively focused, dreamingly open, warmly reminiscent, or ponderingly reflective. Bernard Lonergan's tetrad
might be accomodated here: be attentive (S), be intelligent (N),
be rational (T), be responsible (F).

Not only the homily but the entire structure and flow of liturgical and non-liturgical celebrations may be evaluated and designed in the same way. One of the sources of energy available
for Eucharistic celebration is that, when fittingly celebrated, it
evokes every facet of personality. There is something for the
senses — light and color (candles, vestments), sound (word,
song, music), touch (the gesture of peace), taste (bread and
wine), smell (flowers and incense). There is also something for
the imagination — the symbolism residing in these sense objects and other features such as prophetic or apocalyptic readings. Something for the heart is offered in joyful or sorrowful
songs or in the evocation through the readings or the homily of
the familiar story of Jesus. And there is something for the reflective mind, for example in the readings or in a homily which challenges the congregation to ponder and act on the great issues of
peace and justice. Those ministers who are charged with promoting liturgical life might well ask from time to time: Who comes
to Mass? Who is excited or bored by this or that type of celebration? Other factors, of course, such as age, ethnic culture, and
social class, need to be considered. Our point is that a holistic

appreciation of the diversity of personality types can be helpful
in designing liturgies which will energize people.

Groups and Ministry

A third utility of this model for pastoral life has to do with
group and organizational process. Many ministers have experienced how helpful the Jungian typology can be for improving
their relationships and promoting the effectiveness of their
shared ministry. The Jungian models of group and organizational process shared with many by Management Design, Inc.
has made this a familiar territory for many ministerial teams
which had previously floundered about in the swamps of unor-
ganized or disorganized meetings. It is easier to talk about community and team work than to achieve it. Where ministry is
problematic, I would be inclined to say that the chief problem is
in the ministers, and particularly in their relationships with one
another. As long as there is insensitivity to the diversity and
complementarity of behavioral gifts and preferences, so long
will frustration, oppression, and loss of energy be the name of
the game. No magic formula will ever remove the basic cross
from community or team ministry. But experience shows that
when the understanding of behavioral preferences blends with
a rooting of relationships and structures in the sources of faith,
gifts are disclosed and set free for the good of all.

Perhaps the most helpful language here is the language developed by the ecumenical Church of the Savior in Washington,
D.C. It speaks of the calling forth of gifts present within the community or ministerial team. The opportunities and tensions of
pastoral life call for an integral response, for which the diversity
of gifts contained in all four functions is necessary. It can be
helpful for any ministry team if the preferences and development corresponding to each of the four functions, as well as a
balance of introversion and extraversion, are found within the
group. It is wise policy in seeking staff for a team ministry to
look for the behavioral gifts which may be presently lacking.
The workshops which Magdala, Harold and I have offered may
serve as an example. All three of us share an NF preference, and

we have had to struggle with keeping in touch with the practical side of directing a program. When Jan Futrell joined us for several programs, her sensing gifts added a manifest balance to our corporate effort. But it also provided us with a partner who modelled for us the careful attentiveness to detail which each of us wanted to cultivate within ourself.

I would caution, however, against too simple a response to type imbalance in a ministerial team. A preoccupation with having all functions represented, or with having an equal balance between introverts and extraverts, could lead to stereotyping and "dumping," and to a climate of community where only intuiters were expected to dream, only sensers expected to attend to details, etc. The absence of a person with dominant thinking, for example, can be a spur to all members of a group to develop that gift which, though not preferred, is really present in each member.

This chapter has centered around the Jungian insight that psychic energy is a many-splendored thing, and while each individual is gifted with the full panoply of behavioral gifts, there are identifiable types of persons from the standpoint of basic preferences. Drawing on the solitude/friendship/society model of the preceding chapter, we have seen that all three of these sectors of life provide an arena where an integrated exercise of psychic gifts can mediate the coming of the Kingdom. The individual seeking to grow in the life of the Spirit, and the ministry team seeking to make that Spirit contagious, can be helped by a consistent use of this model.

Questions for Reflection

For personal spirituality:

1. With or without the help of the MBTI, are you in touch with your preferred ways of taking in reality and in turn shaping it? For example, would you say you are more practical than imaginative, more a heart person than a head person, more introverted than extraverted?

2. What are some of the implications of your answers to the above questions for your prayer, relationships, and work?
3. At the present stage of your life, are you conscious of any inner call to develop some new facet of your personality?

For pastoral ministry:

1. What personal gifts do you bring to your ministry?
2. What psychological avoidances and attachments do you have to be wary of as you minister to and with others?
3. How might your ministry team or other communal efforts be helped by applying the model discussed in this chapter?

4
Action/Contemplation

Back about 1973, I took part in a workshop at Dunwoodie, the New York archdiocesan seminary in Yonkers. About fifty sisters and priests engaged in urban ministry had gathered to talk about the place of prayer in their demanding service of the poor. I was asked to speak on action and contemplation. I remember that Monsignor Bob Fox, who had worked in Harlem at the time of the riots in the middle sixties, and Father Lou Gigante, another veteran of urban parish ministry and at one time a council member in New York City, spoke from rich experiences of a ministry which I knew only vicariously. At the conclusion of the weekend Fathers Phil Murnion and Bob Imbelli and I agreed to meet regularly in order to explore some implications of the workshop for an American spirituality. Meeting faithfully for more than two years, we arrived at a preliminary draft of six chapters for a collaborative work that never did see the light of publication. But these conversations were a great enrichment and encouragement for me, as was a weekend meeting at Ventnor, New Jersey, arranged by Sister Margaret Dowling. There Bob Imbelli, Bill Callahan, Sister Mary Daniel Turner, and several Sisters of Charity, helped to keep the theme in the forefront of my consciousness. Since then I have used this material in a score of talks and workshops. Several years ago Bob Heyer invited me to write an essay for an issue of *New Catholic World* on American spirituality and I seized the opportunity to lay out this model in print.[1]

The Dunwoodie workshop was far from being the first time that the theme of action/contemplation had engaged my interest. My fascination for it dates back to my novitiate at St. Andrew-on-Hudson at Poughkeepsie in 1941. There we were exposed to the dictum of St. Ignatius about finding God in all

things and all things in God. There too I first heard Jerome
Nadal's characterization of our holy founder as being a contemplative in action. A fellow Jesuit, Joe Conwell, with whom I
studied in Rome in the early 1950s, had done his doctoral disser-
tation, subsequently published, on this theme. And, finally, I benefited from a dialogue in the late 1970s at the Quixote Center
in Washington, where a dozen people dialogued and then published in tabloid form a set of essays, *The Wind Is Rising: Prayer
Ways for Active People*. Most of the essays touched on the action-
contemplation theme, and Bill Callahan's contribution con-
sisted of a first sketch of his concept of "noisy contemplation."

For the following reflection it is also important to say that,
from the beginning, my insight into action/contemplation was
interwoven with a broader theme, derived from Karl Rahner's
theology of grace, namely that prayer in the most basic sense is
identical with faith, and indeed *is* faith as a dimension of graced
consciousness. I became convinced that this Rahnerian insight
was an appropriate, and perhaps necessary, foundation for the
pardigm shift which I was proposing on the classic theme of contemplation and action. Hence the following reflection has two
parts, dealing respectively with faith/prayer and with action/
contemplation.

Prayer is Conscious Faith

We may say of prayer what the *Imitation of Christ* says of
compunction: it is better to experience it than to define it.
Strictly speaking, prayer is not definable at all. Prayer is not
merely reflection, introspection, meditation. It stands too much
within the mystery of God's life in us to admit of proper definition. There are indeed some classic formulations. Teresa of
Avila described it as a conversation with God by whom we know
we are loved. The catechism used to speak of prayer as the raising of the mind and heart to God for purposes of adoration,
thanksgiving, forgiveness, and petition.

As I have mentioned, my own understanding of prayer has
been shaped by Karl Rahner's theology of grace. It brilliantly

links the theological and spiritual tradition of faith as a conscious experience of God with a philosophical and theological anthropology which distinguishes a transcendent dimension of human behavior from a more categorical or "thematic" dimension. The distinction functions extensively in Rahner's theology, for example, in his well known conception of "anonymous Christianity."

For Rahner, each human being in every instance of truly human behavior is being addressed by God in a self-revelation and self-gift that is mediated through some human value. Wherever a person is confronted with a situation of moral choice, the possibility of an act of saving faith exists. Even where the thought of God is absent from thematic consciousness, this offer of grace and a positive or negative response to it stands within consciousness, at a deeper or more transcendent level.

Since I am using this Rahnerian thesis solely as a foundation for saying something more, I will not argue for it or attempt to clarify it further. Accepting it as at least a plausible hypothesis, I would take the further step of saying that every exercise of faith, hope, and charity is also, in the transcendent dimension of consciousness, an exercise of radical prayer. To put it in headline fashion, *prayer is faith in the dimension of consciousness.* Such an assertion, it seems to me, extends and formulates a long Christian tradition which spoke of praying always and finding God in all things. That tradition also distinguished formal prayer from habitual or virtual prayer. I am not suggesting that what I call here transcendental prayer is simply another name for habitual or virtual prayer. The latter probably requires at least a dim presence in thematic consciousness of an awareness of God. Still, assuming the validity of the Rahnerian anthropology, I find it congruous to interpret the Christian ideal of praying without ceasing in the light of Rahner's insight into the gracing of human consciousness.

Does this mean that all that we do is prayer? Yes, but only *if,* and to the degree that, what I do is an exercise of faith. What a big if! It is only in the measure that my "ordinary" behavior is an exercise of faith that it achieves the status of radical prayer. Later, in speaking of action, I will return to the question of the conditions required if our human behavior is to be truly action, genuinely faith, and so worthy of the name of prayer.

Action: Contemplative and Responsive

With this base, the identification of prayer with the exercise of faith, we can move on to the second part of this reflection, and deal directly with the traditional theme of contemplation and action. The literature of spirituality contains thousands of volumes which seek to help us pray. But how many readers can name more than one or two spiritual books whose explicit aim is to help us understand what it means to act? Largely because of an underlying anthropology — somewhat dualistic in its tendencies — the spiritual tradition has followed, for the most part, a "trickle down" model of the relationship of contemplation and action.

This can be illustrated from the common understanding of three celebrated formulas: 1) the Benedictine *ora et labora* (prayer and work); 2) the Dominican *contemplari et contemplata aliis tradere* (contemplate, then share with others the fruits of contemplation); 3) the Ignatian *simul in actione contemplativus* (at once a contemplative in action).

Like all theological axioms and formulas, these three carry with them the flavor of their cultural origins. "Prayer and work" takes us back to the circle of monastic life, and to the regular hourly, daily, weekly, monthly, and yearly rhythms of that life, so attuned to the rhythms of nature. The Dominican formula also suggests a recurring rhythm, only this time between the domestic and apostolic poles of a vocation to proclaim the Good News that had first been contemplatively savored by the preacher in the common life of the priory. "Contemplation in action" had its origin within the turn to modernity of the late Renaissance and the Reformation, a period when the patternless exploration of new realms provided a new root metaphor for the spiritual journey.

Note a few things about these three beautiful and still valuable phrases. In each of them, even the third, work or action was somehow derivative. The starting point, the energizing center, was prayer, contemplation. What was imperative with respect to action was that it be contemplative, prayerful, that it participate in the qualities found more perfectly in contemplative union with God. Contemplation of itself was viewed as God-referent; work, ministry, action, was so only derivatively. The primary encounter with God was conceived to take place in times and spaces apart. In the popular mind, at least, the flow of spiritual energy was unidirectional, from contemplation to action. Contemplation stored up the energy which was then expended in action. Prayer was, in Dom Chautard's classic work, *The Soul of the Apostolate*, the one source of ministerial energy. What apostolic encounter with God did for prayer was largely neglected. The possibility that, as Matthew 25:31-46 more than hints, the primary encounter with God might take place in meeting the needs of the neighbor, does not seem to have occurred in this "trickle down" outlook.

But suppose one rearranges the mode, shifts the paradigm? Suppose we begin our search for understanding not with contemplation but with action? Within our modern, and especially within our North American context, something new and distinctive may emerge if we first ask what it means to act. With a nod to more profound treatments of action, especially that of Maurice Blondel, I would begin by saying that not every instance of human behavior or activity is worthy of the noble name of action. I would distinguish genuine action from illusory and addictive behavior. Whenever, and to the extent that, I really act humanly, I am, first of all, *aware* of what I am doing. Both Marxist and Freudian currents of thought have helped to alert us to how much self-deception, flight from truth, illusion, inhabit our daily behavior. Jesus prayed on the cross, "Father, forgive them. They don't know what they are doing" (Luke 23:34). Is this not, tragically, a daily portrait of humans dwelling in the darkness of illusion, particularly under the spell of cultural stereotypes, manipulations, and ideologies? In contrast, genuine action takes place when, and to the degree that, people accept the enlightening gift of the Spirit and so become what they are doing. This, then, is a first quality of genuine action. It takes place in the full light of awareness.

Second, genuine action happens when, through the same gift of the Spirit, people do what they really want to do; that is, freely choose to act humanly. In this aspect genuine action is contrasted with compulsive, addictive, or unfree behavior. Paul summarized this pitiful condition in simple but eloquent terms: "I find myself doing what I really don't want to do, and not doing what I really want" (Romans 7:15). How better to express the deadly dynamism of sin, in which illusion and addiction reinforce and feed on one another? Human sinfulness differs radically from the angelic clarity and freedom which marked the sin of Lucifer in the myth of creation, and even from the sin of our first parents in paradise in the same myth. We humans are never in a tranquil situation of angelic or paradisal light and freedom.

Salvation comes to us only in solidarity with the second Adam, whose grace bears the mark of the Cross. The only light we know is a victory over darkness. Our freedom comes only by way of liberation from enslavement. Genuine human action will always bear the mark of conflict and conquest.

If action is such, what then is contemplation? Drawing on the same anthropology, we can distinguish two phases in the rhythm of integral action. The awareness of which I have spoken is really a receptivity or openness to the real, both human and divine. It is aptly termed contemplation, or the contemplative dimension of integral action. It is accompanied by a responsive dimension, a saying of Yes to values, and hence to God, in the free willing of what we really want. Whenever faith/prayer is exercised, this awareness/freedom is simultaneously both contemplative and responsive.

It follows then that: 1) *all action is contemplative*, provided and in the degree that it is really action; 2) *all contemplation* (in the traditional sense) *is a form of action*, provided and in the degree that it is truly contemplative. This model refuses to say, then, that we are sometimes contemplating and sometimes acting. All action has a contemplative dimension. Within such a paradigm, it is clear, the notion of action has been broadened so that it is conceptually inclusive of both contemplative and responsive components. The paradigm in effect disengages us from the usual positing of a polar relationship between contemplation and action. Instead, it gives the term action a comprehensive sense, comprising a contemplative and responsive pole.

Special Times and Spaces

But if all action is contemplative, is there any need for contemplation in the traditional sense, that is, times and spaces apart when we open ourselves to God's action within us? Yes, there is. In the new paradigm, however, there is less danger of conceiving such special contemplative situations as the only ones in which we meet God contemplatively. There is less danger too of missing the fact that both in such special situations and in the rest of our lives we live according to a rhythm of receptivity and response.

The times and spaces apart retain their necessity and importance for two reasons. First of all, there is the pragmatic reason that we need to *practice* finding God in all things. What happens when we practice anything — golf or typing, dancing or praying — is that we create a special environment free from pressure and distraction so that the best of our energies can be invested in the learning process. The quip about not being able to walk and chew gum at the same time has a real point to it, especially when there is a question of engaging the deeper parts of ourselves simultaneously in the search for God and the fulfillment of human tasks and relationships.

Were we angelic or paradisal creatures living in full innocence, finding God in all things would be effortless and unambiguous. As progeny of a sinful Adam and Eve, however, we are prone to self-deception, unfreedom, idolatry. The road to enlightenment and liberation takes strenuous effort. We need to learn by deliberate practice, in favorable environments, the ways of the Kingdom. We need also to conceive our times and spaces apart dynamically, as integral to the building of the habit of contemplative/responsive action, which we hope to exercise with greater facility, even under the pressures of social and professional life. In this sense, the fruit and criterion of formal prayer is virtual prayer. The steady practice of action in chosen environments (formal prayer) will over a period of years yield a greater facility in acting in imposed environments (virtual prayer).

Speaking in this way could make it appear that formal prayer is a mere tool. This would, of course, frustrate the very character of prayer as a deep, loving relationship with God which is its own end. This is where the second reason for moments apart comes into play. Just as our human relationships of love and friendship bring a spontaneous desire to be with those whom we love, so the yearning for God will, as it grows, carry with it the desire to be with the loved one in environments which foster deep communion in awareness and freedom. Precisely because our concupiscent cultural environments of everyday living are infected with illusion and addiction, the seriousness of our search for God will be signalized by our will to seek God at times in situations of leisure. "Noisy contemplation" will be less cacophonous for Christians as they learn, within the basic rhythm of contemplative/responsive action, to find the appropriate interplay of engagement/disengagement with respect to daily routines and pressures.

Practical Spirituality

What are some of the practical consequences for spirituality and ministry of this action-centered model? The most basic import has to do with the conservation and utilization of psychic and spiritual energy. Each of us can testify, on the basis of experience, to the healthiness of a tension between formal prayer and other activities in our lives. But we also, I believe, experience a considerable loss of energy because we tend to look upon formal prayer as the only source of spiritual energy, a lonely filling station along the highway through the desert. We tend to demand of those times and spaces apart more power and nurture than they are capable of bestowing. We also miss the strength and vitality that can come from meeting God in the very exercise of ministry and indeed in all of our activities outside of formal prayer. Because of the language bias which invites us to seek in formal prayer alone the sources of the energy which we are conceived to expend in our activities, we waste countless opportunities given by God for renewing our strength like eagles.

When we change the paradigm to one of contemplative and responsive action verified in all that we do — with the big proviso that what we do be done in faith — we are encouraged to tap into the energy resources which await us in every nook and cranny of daily life.

In the limit case of energy loss — what we have come to call burnout — our model can provide a theological base for effective strategies, both preventative and recuperative. The common strategy for warding off burnout is to build more leisure into an overly busy life. This is good and necessary, but it is not all we can do. We need also a sustained and direct effort to enhance the contemplative dimension of our investment in ministry, profession, work. Correspondingly, we need to look upon prayer not merely as a time to get our breath before plunging again into activity, but as one specific and important context in which we exercise ourselves in the rhythm of contemplation and response. In general, what needs to yield is the gulf between prayer — or what we are accustomed to call prayer — and everything else we do. When the idea of contemplative/responsive action becomes embodied within our attitudes and convictions, as well as in concrete strategies and tactics, we are on the road to dealing effectively with ministerial burnout. More positively, we are growing towards a Christian life which is always, as a life of faith, both contemplative and responsive.

Strategies and tactics are crucial, of course. The principal vehicles for building this model into our lives is probably the "consciousness examen," which I have already mentioned in Chapter 2. As I make myself present, in imagination or silent awareness, both retrospectively and prospectively, to the scenes in my daily life, I seek in God's presence to be in touch with both the contemplative and the responsive facets of my behavior. Looking back on the day as it comes to a close, I ask: Where and how did God come to me? Did I recognize God's presence? If not, what hindered me? Anxiety, neurotic craving, fear of others, etc? And how did I respond? What shaped my response — a true movement of the Spirit, or one or other form of personal or societal concupiscence? More generally, what was the level of my awareness, my freedom, on this particular day of the Lord? Such an exercise of memory, with gratitude and compunction, can lead into an exercise of imagination and hope that tomorrow will be a better day. I can anticipate tomorrow's situations, see myself being contemplative and responsive, alert myself to hazards and obstacles to genuine action, and pray for grace to be alive and free when I enter the envisaged situations.

Over a period of months and years, we can build up through the consciousness examen a living bridge between formal and virtual prayer. If it is not oversimplifying the matter, we might say that our need is to become more contemplative in our "ordinary" activities, and more responsive in time of formal prayer. Even more, we need to become convinced that all action is contemplative, in the degree that it is action, and that all contemplation is a form of action, in the degree that it is contemplative.

Responsive Ministry

Now let me add a word about the implications of the present model for ministry. In the first chapter I indicated that the goal of ministry might be conceived in terms of power and energy. Something similar may be said here. Apart from any specific Christian content, our ministry will be effective to the degree that we help people become aware of what is really happening in their total behavior, and be gradually freed for a true and integral response to life. When Christians, or any human beings, know what they are doing; and when they do what they really want to do, they are fulfilling in their lives the kingdom of God. In the Western world there is no greater threat to our humanity than the narcotizing of awareness and the crippling of freedom through the manipulative and numbing impact of the prevailing culture. The Christian churches, through the enlightening and liberating Gospel entrusted to their stewardship, are being called as never before in history to stand for all that is human. If ministry is a contagion, then only ministers who have been infected with the Gospel call to action are capable of drawing others to action that is both contemplative and responsive. To the degree, for example, that a parish staff — whatever its good intentions and good works — succumbs to the work ethic in its obscuring of vision and blunting of freedom, that staff becomes inept for the role of modelling and leading the community toward genuine evangelical action.

Finally, let me link this chapter with the two immediately preceding ones. The Walden model, when brought into contact with the theme of action, can remind us that the action of individuals is never isolated from interpersonal and societal influences. The consciousness examen might profitably at times attend to the helps and hindrances to genuine action which come from our personal associations and particularly from the surrounding culture. If we are in a family or religious community, for example, where the common life affords little time and space for what is truly contemplative, our personal struggle becomes even more difficult. The choices which we make as individuals for enlarging our capacity for genuine action need to be made with awareness of such influences. Conversely, when a community has come to a good level of dialogue and sharing, its agenda might well include attention to the balance of the contemplative and the responsive within the common life, as well as an evaluation of the impact of the surrounding culture on the life of the community. In similar fashion readers may wish to reflect on ways in which the model of solitude/friendship/society and the model of contemplative/responsive action might come together in their lives.

Little needs to be said about linking the model of the four Jungian functions with the present model. In Chapter 3 I already noted that the perceiving functions, sensing and intuiting, correspond to the contemplative side of personality, while the judging functions, thinking and feeling, are responsive in character. Growth towards individuation through the development of the less favored functions necessarily implies growth in balancing the contemplative and responsive elements in our total action.

Questions for Reflection

For personal spirituality:

1. What do I think about the basic model of contemplative/responsive action described in this chapter?
2. In what ways am I still one of those who "don't know what they are doing?" In what ways do I find myself "doing what I really don't want to do, and not doing what I really want?"
3. How would I describe the relationship, actual and desired, between formal and virtual prayer in my life?

For ministry:

1. Do I, with my associates in ministry, model for those we serve, the contagious awareness and freedom of which this chapter speaks?
2. What practical measures might help our ministerial team and those we serve to grow in the capacity for genuine action?
3. Have we dealt effectively, through dialogue and policy, with the danger of burnout?

5

The Ignatian Exercises

My first exposure to the Spiritual Exercises of St. Ignatius took place during my student days at Xavier High School and St. Peter's College (Jersey City), both Jesuit institutions. The Exercises meant practically nothing to me, however, until I met Fr. Albert Heald, a just ordained Franciscan Friar of the Atonement, in the winter of 1938-39. We were both convalescing from tuberculosis at a little "cure cottage" in Saranac Lake run by the Sisters of Mercy. Fr. Albert had recently made his ordination retreat under a Canadian Jesuit, Lacouture, whose austere (Jansenistic, his critics claimed) interpretation of the Spiritual Exercises had occasioned remarkable conversions in some priests and bitter opposition from others. Incidentally, through Fr. John Hugo, a Pittsburgh priest, the Lacouture spirituality was to become significant in the journey of faith of Dorothy Day. In 1985, Fr. Hugo, back in Pittsburgh, was still giving "the retreat," and my brother Jim (Fr. Martin de Porres, a Capuchin), went out to make one, in a kind of nostalgia trip which brought him back to the days when, as a fireman in New York City, he first came to know Dorothy Day and the Catholic Worker. But back to my own journey of conversion. Fr. Albert's persistent evangelization and God's grace, working especially through the abstract logic of the Ignatian "Principle and Foundation," eventually brought me, at twenty, to an exciting new outlook on life. My becoming a Jesuit in 1941 was primarily the result not of the eight years I had spent with Jesuits in Xavier High School and St. Peter's College, but rather of those several months at Saranac Lake when God called to me through the zeal of Fr. Albert and the highly rational appeal of the Principle and Foundation. I never completely abandoned this somewhat philosophical model of salvation, although subsequent exposure to more ge-

71

nial spiritual writers like Dietrich von Hildebrand and Gerald
Vann, and later to Pierre Teilhard de Chardin and Karl Rahner,
led me to appreciate that the Lacouture model was, like all models, a limited guide which also contained serious risks.

Years of subsequent exposure to the Spiritual Exercises
brought me to marvel at the remarkable blend in them of two
strands, one rational, pragmatic, and purposeful, and the other
more contemplative, playful, and intuitive. I expressed this perception in an article in the *Review for Religious* in 1972.[1] A good
deal of the momentum for writing it had come from reading the
insightful linking of Aquinas and Heidegger by Fred Crowe,
with whom I had studied in Rome in the 1950s.[2] Later I will
summarize Fred's contribution to my understanding of the
Exercises. Not long after, I applied the distinction of societal sin
and societal grace to the Spiritual Exercises in an essay in
Studies in the Spirituality of the Jesuits.[3] Then, in 1976, in a
talk given and published in the Philippines, I suggested that the
Spiritual Exercises were not only a retreat manual, but in effect
were basic to all Jesuit life and ministry. A few years later a project of the Woodstock Theological Center, which found publication in 1979, saw me trying to apply the Ignatian principles of
discernment to the choices made by committed Christians
within public life.[4] Finally, when I was asked to give a paper at
a symposium at Regis College in Toronto in 1980, my interest in
the world food and hunger situation — which I had explored in
a paper for a human rights project at the Woodstock Theological
Center — led me to examine some of the implications of the almost totally neglected "Rules with Regard to Eating" of the
Spiritual Exercises.[5] Here I was concerned — and excited —
about overcoming a certain fundamentalism which I had perceived among some Jesuits in their interpretation of our origins.
The rather quaint (by our standards) "Rules with Regard to Eating" gave me an attractive test case for applying to the Exercises
some of the hermeneutical principles which Biblical scholars
had solidly established in making the Scriptures fully available
to us again.

As I began to write the present book, it occurred to me that my understanding of the Spiritual Exercises had been shaped in large part by all the models which I have thus far exhibited. So the following reflections offer not so much another model as a journey through the Exercises, making use of the models outlined in the first four chapters.

The Power of Ignatius

What accounts for the remarkable power of the Spiritual Exercises for over four centuries in the life of the Church? History testifies that, from the period of the Counter Reformation until today, they have been the sustaining heart of the Society of Jesus as well as a force of rare efficacy within the spiritual life of the whole Church. When one looks at the book of the Exercises, one finds, for the most part, a set of dull and prosaic suggestions for directors and retreatants. Only rarely, in some of the "key exercises" such as the Kingdom of Christ, Two Standards, and Contemplation for Gaining Divine Love, does one come across a hint of the enormous power which the book — or rather the shared spiritual experience which the book describes and assists — has exerted.

What accounts for such remarkable power? There are several answers to this question, all of them partial and plausible. The one which I propose here is based on the models of spiritual growth which have been examined in the preceding pages, and on some other convictions which I have come to entertain about the Spiritual Exercises.

I think we may say that, even compared with other great saints and founders, Ignatius of Loyola was a Christian in whose personality and spiritual physiognomy power and energy were especially prominent. He was, as he admitted in the self-description of his *Autobiography*, essentially a pilgrim, indeed a passionate pilgrim intent on reaching the holy shrine, the heavenly Jerusalem, accompanied by as great a throng of human beings as possible. Of the two contrasting spiritual symbols, the temple or dwelling and the way or the journey, it was clearly the latter which represented his call and that of his disci-

ples. From Loyola to Montserrat to Manresa to Jerusalem to
Paris to Venice to Rome, first in solitary pilgrimage, then in
companionship, and finally as an ecclesiastical leader, life for
him was essentially a journey and a mission. While the last
years of his life found him, in body, immobile at the center of the
institutional Church, his dwelling there was, in its spirit, the opposite of sedentary as he presided over the constant comings
and goings of rapidly growing numbers of Jesuits. An Italian
Jesuit, Mario Scaduto, has graphically depicted the excitement
and the dangers of this life on *la strada*, the roads of Italy and of
the Western world, in the first decades of the Society of Jesus.

It was no accident, I think, that the favorite Marian devotion
of Ignatius himself and of Jesuits to this day has been to the
Madonna della Strada — our Lady of the Way, or the Highway,
or the Street. The distinctive energy of Jesuit life has to do with
mission, with the process of hearing and saying, "Go forth," ut-
tered over and over again to one another by companions in
Jesus. That is why efforts from whatever source to monasticize
the life of apostolic religious is experienced by Jesuits, today no
less than in the period of our origins, as a sinister threat to the
Ignatian charism.

Along with this quality of immense apostolic energy Ignatius
had a keen sense of, and appreciation for, power. What I have
said in Chapter 1 about the importance of a positive estimate of
human power is exemplified in him. The Principle and Foundation is the sober utterance of someone who is determined to put
all human resources to their maximum use. The well-known
fourth vow of Jesuits, a special commitment of obedience to the
Pope in special missions which he may entrust to the Society of
Jesus, has its foundation in the conviction of Ignatius that the
Roman pontiff, as vicar of Christ and successor of St. Peter, is in
a unique position to further the world-wide glory of God. For Ignatius, what is primary in the Church is not that it is Roman
but that it is catholic. It was its catholicity which gave to its
romanitá the force which drew the devotion of this power-sensi-
tive saint. To be close to the principal human vehicle of divine
power in the Church, as Ignatius conceived it, was a choice that

was both mystical and pragmatic.

The Spiritual Exercises embody both the spiritual journey and the spiritual physiognomy of Ignatius. One might expect to find in them the strong accent on power and energy which was so characteristic of their author. Such is indeed the case. With no attempt at detailed analysis, here are some of the aspects of the Spiritual Exercises which illustrate this.

The Power of Method

Next to the living faith which is their power center, the principal factor in the amazing efficacy of the Exercises is something quite prosaic — their *method*, or rather, the very fact that they provide a method for anyone who is seeking God's will. The first sentence of the "annotations" with which Ignatius begins the text defines spiritual exercises as consisting in any method or way (*modo*) of examining one's conscience, meditating, etc. Recall that the term "method" has its root in the Greek term *hodos*, which means road, and you will better appreciate the link between the Ignatian journey and the Ignatian insistence on method. Bernard Lonergan was not the first Jesuit to gain the insight that appropriate method was a key to power and energy. It was given to Ignatius to see that the immense resources of the person making the Exercises could be squandered unless both retreatant and director paid constant attention to method and structure in the experience of prayer.

Of numerous instances of attention to method, I would single out one which is extremely simple but quite important. It is the framework of 1) disposition (or "composition"), 2) experience, and 3) reflection, which Ignatius proposes for each exercise. The experience of meeting God in prayer will be richer, he saw, as the one who prays is ready — in body, psyche, and spirit — for the encounter, and as the experience itself is reflectively assimilated by the whole person at the end of the prayer. In both preparation and review Ignatius has the retreatant pay careful attention to the place and time of prayer, to bodily posture and mental alertness, and above all to spiritual dispositions such as reverence and familiarity. He is vigilant too in cautioning the director not to encumber the retreatant with an excess of material, but to leave the latter free to receive from God what God chooses to give. Similarly, the conclusion of each period of formal prayer is a time for reflection, for savoring the experience, and for letting it enter more deeply and abidingly into the spiritual posture and tonality of the retreatant.

One could list at length other directives which touch on method: preliminary prayers and preludes, colloquies and repetitions, changes of strategy when the search for God seems blocked, engaging in or refraining from penitential practices, etc.

It need hardly be said that method is a key to power and energy not so much by generating them as by conserving and directing them. His own faith experience had taught the saint where power and energy flow — in the highly personal and intimate dialogue of creature with creator, enlightened by Scripture as read in the Church and embodied in the humanity of Jesus Christ. Method did not create these living waters, but it provided channels for them to refresh the thirsty soil of the spirit.

It is quite likely that this insistence on method stemmed from a personality trait of Ignatius which was also responsible for other features of the Spiritual Exercises, notably for their preoccupation with *order and disorder*. The Exercises aim, Ignatius tells us twice, in the first annotation (SE n. 1) and in the title (SE n. 21), at the overcoming of disorderly affections, so that the retreatant may make a decision which is in keeping with God's will.

Both as theme and as structuring element, right order is pivotal in the movement of the Spiritual Exercises. The Principle and Foundation offers not so much a set of points for meditation as a basic context and presupposition for all the following exercises. This powerful paragraph is a detached outline of what an orderly Christian life looks like. It names the *goal* (the praise, reverence, and service of God and the salvation of one's soul), the *means* to the goal (all creatures), the *rule* for right order regarding the means (use when they help, abstain when they hinder), and the basic *disposition* required if the rule is to be effectively followed (total indifference or inner freedom). The spirit of the Principle and Foundation, one of purposive adjustment of means to ends, pervades the directives for the retreat itself. The time and fare of meals, sleep and exercise, posture in prayer, lingering with or moving on from particular prayer material, and an endless series of other particulars, are dealt with out of a preoccupation with right order. That such order is to be flexible only enhances this insistence — a fixed ultimate purpose dictates and guides the relativizing of intermediate goals.

Functions in the Exercises

From what has been said thus far, it seems quite clear that, so far as the Jungian functions are concerned, the thinking function was well exercised by the author of the Spiritual Exercises. I would not venture here even to guess what Ignatius' personality type might have been. One would need a wider base, including his autobiography and journal, his letters and the Constitutions of the Society of Jesus, to ground even an informed speculation. One would also have to deal with the question of whether the manifestations of the thinking function in the text of the Spiritual Exercises might possibly correspond not with the preferences but with the shadow side of their author's personality. And one would have to reckon with the possible paradox, if it is that, that this strong thinking personality had power to elicit deep feeling from the thousands of retreatants who have experienced conversion of heart through the Spiritual Exercises.

Whatever type may have been verified in Ignatius, the instrument he created serves to discountenance any tendency to banish rationality from even the deepest mystical experience. More positively, I would suggest that the power of the Exercises for fostering deep conversion in all types of personality is due to the fact that they offer something significant to each of the four functions, and contain sufficient flexibility to keep this or that type from being forced into a Procustean bed. It seems worth while to linger with this model for a moment. Having made some observations about thinking, let me comment on the other three functions as finding a place in the text and in the process of the Spiritual Exercises.

If sensing is seen as a focused perception that is attentive to present particulars, it is clearly honored in the Exercises. The text is made up, as we have seen, largely of minutiae touching the time given to meals, sleep, and attendance at Church services; the preliminary steps prior to each exercise; and even the formula of the prayer to be offered without exception at the beginning of the exercise. Such a preoccupation on the part of Ignatius speaks to the concerns especially of an ISTJ or ISFJ type (to use the MBTI code), which fulfills conscientiously the detailed prescriptions of the appointed task. On the other hand, the invitation to contemplate the Gospel scenes in a dreaming, affective, participatory manner seems geared especially to another sensing type, designated as ISFP, whose sensing is less ordered to the fulfillment of needs or responsibilities to others than to present enjoyment. Ignatius presents the Gospel scenes which are to be contemplated with a terseness and simplicity of expression which is clearly characteristic of the sensing function. As with thinking, one might justifiably be led to guess that we are dealing with the work of someone with a clear preference for sensing over intuiting. I would not venture such a speculation. But, as far as the text of the Spiritual Exercises is concerned, we can say that its dominant tone is simple, practical, and matter of fact, even when it advocates the use of imagination by the retreatant. In any case, Ignatius would have the retreatant exercise sensing and live in the present moment of the experience without worrying about what might be ahead (SE n. 11).

He also, however, calls forth the gifts represented by the intuitive function, notably imagination and fantasy, as well as the symbol-making power of the retreatant. His own experience at Manresa contained some quite remarkable imaginative visions. There is no doubt that he was led by the Spirit to dream great dreams of what he might accomplish for the kingdom of Christ. Both of these aspects of his conversion experience found their way into the suggestions he offered retreatants. Morton Kelsey, in *The Other Side of Silence*, an effort to rehabilitate the role of active imagination in prayer, cites Ignatius in support of his advocacy. Though the text of the Exercises is, as we have said, sober and terse, it invites the retreatant to a free play of imagination by entering participatively into the mysteries being contemplated. The energies required for free and courageous decision are gathered for the most part not through highly rational motivational principles — though these are by no means absent or unimportant, and find a place in the directives on the times and modes of making an election — but through the play of nostalgic imagination on the mysteries of the Gospel. Then, prospectively, special exercises such as the Kingdom of Christ and Two Standards evoke the use of the intuitive function by asking the retreatant to envisage new possibilities of dedicated service.

Symbol, closely associated with the intuitive function, enables us to go beyond the actual and the concrete to what these intimate to our third eye, our sixth sense. Of the many evocations of the symbolic in the Spiritual Exercises, a typical one is the fourth point of the Contemplation for Gaining Divine Love. Here Ignatius has the retreatant consider that all our human blessings and gifts, such as power, justice, goodness, and mercy, "descend from above as the rays of light descend from the sun, and as the waters flow from the fountains, etc." (SE n. 237). One thinks here of that son of Ignatius, Gerard Manley Hopkins, for whom "inscape," a special perception of the beyond as present in the singular beauty of each person, thing, or encounter, was a way both poetic and spiritual of "finding God in all things."

These various exercises of imagination are joined in the Exercises to the exercise of the feeling function. The contemplations of the mysteries are exercises of affectivity in the remembrance of love shown, and the aspirations contained in the key exercises are penetrated with a yearning love for Jesus Christ. The grace sought through all the contemplations of the second, third, and fourth "weeks" is the grace of *intimacy*. The loving relationship to Christ in his mysteries carries with it the assimilation through discipleship of his values. Both intimacy and values are terms which point to the feeling function.

Thus do all four functions find their place in the experience of the Spiritual Exercises. If the text as such seems to accent sensing and thinking, it invites to a prayer which may be tilted in the direction of intuiting and feeling. This is an oversimplification, of course (committed, by the way, by one who is tilted in the same direction). For example, in the immediate context of the "election," Ignatius provides for a good deal of calm, sober reflection and for some practical procedures. In any case, I think I have said enough to suggest what a more detailed study might corroborate, namely that the power of the Spiritual Exercises to foster deep and lasting change in the lives of individual Christians derives in part from their ability to enlist the resources of all four aspects of the human personality, as described in the Jungian typology.

Contemplation and Response

Clearly related to this psychological aspect of the Spiritual Exercises is the way in which they embody the rhythm of contemplation and response which I have described in the previous chapter. From the vantage point of what was said there, we may now say that the making of an Ignatian retreat is a distinctive experience of Christian action in which contemplative and responsive forms and postures of prayer alternate in an energizing harmony and tension. This was the original point I wished to make in the *Review for Religious* article. I will not repeat in detail what I said there. The principal insight that I found in Ignatius was the realization that the most powerful force in practical decision is the interplay of intuitive and affective contemplation, which seems furthest removed from anything practical. The personal charism of Ignatius included a lived sense of the dialectical movement of reality, and he was keenly aware that it is the apparently wasted moments of life, the engagement in *il dolce far niente* (the sweet doing of nothing), which contain the most important energies for shaping life through basic options.

In the essay I drew upon what Fred Crowe had written as he linked St. Thomas' analysis of the dynamism of intellect and will with Heidegger's distinction of *complacency* and *concern*. Fred's insight into the "complacency" which is at the source of "concern" helped me to appreciate the contemplative dimension of action:

> Before there is the Christian imperative, the exhortation to conversion and change, there must come first the Christian indicative, the celebration of the change which God in Christ has already wrought in human life. Before there is struggling, hopeful concern and purposeful action into the future, there must be grateful memory of the mighty deed of God our Father in raising Jesus from the dead; there must be recollection of the gift of the Spirit and the love of God for us poured forth in our hearts. Before we go forth in peace to love and serve the Lord, we must first celebrate the Lord's love for us. Before we do, we must be. Before we function, we must exist. Before we play a role, we must be a person. Before there is purpose in our lives, there must be meaning. Before love can give, it must first receive. Before we breathe forth love on the world, we must breathe in the Spirit of God.[6]

Such an accent in the statement of the dialectical tension between the contemplative and the responsive dimensions of action does not at all deny what was said in the previous chapter, namely that there is a *mutual* interdependence of the two components of action. It does, however, affirm the primacy of God's action. Within our Western technological culture it calls attention to the shallowness of any mere pragmatism (and any attendant activism) which would neglect the immense energies in the contemplative side of our humanity.

Solitude and Companionship

A further source of the power and energy present in the

Spiritual Exercises consists in the deep solitude on which they insist, while allowing and providing for the contribution to be made, in the language of the Walden model, by both friendship and society. The Walden model described in Chapter 2 fits both the personal journey of Ignatius and the Spiritual Exercises which socialized that journey.

It is interesting to look at the paths taken by Ignatius after his conversion within the framework of solitude, friendship, and society. Without strain we can distinguish three successive periods. During the first he was drawn for several years to a predominantly solitary life. For a while, in fact, he considered whether God was calling him to be a Carthusian. He became in effect, as Jean Leclercq once described him, a wandering monk within a special Christian tradition. He deliberately chose to journey to Jerusalem without a companion, that he might have God alone as his support. In the second, friendship became predominant in the way his spiritual journey was accented. First in Spain, then in Paris where he studied for a number of years, his vision and way of life became contagious among disciples, with some of whom he forged enduring bonds, especially through giving them the Exercises. When in 1535 the time had come for his band (who made vows together at Montmartre in 1534) to carry out a common resolve, they went to Italy, ministered in various towns and cities, and discerned their further comradeship. "Friends in the Lord" is the way that this interpersonal stage of Ignatius' journey has been described. Finally, once it became clear that God was calling them to be an enduring community specially related to the Pope, they elected Ignatius as official leader, and he entered into what we may consider a predominantly societal phase of his existence. Rome, the heart of the institutional Church, was to claim him until his death in 1556. Much of this time was spent in writing for his community, as it began to grow towards becoming the worldwide Society of Jesus, Constitutions which would provide it with appropriate structures for its journey through the centuries. From the first, Ignatius' vision and life-style had been ecclesial; now it became ecclesiastical.

In addition to providing a framework for interpreting Ignatius' life, the Walden triad can serve also as a beacon for Jesuits as disciples of Ignatius. An integral life for us, as for members of other Christian communities, is one in which the energies deriving from solitude, friendship, and society are kept in a balanced and dynamic tension. In this effort we are helped not a little by making the Ignatian Exercises, which contain all three kinds of energy.

There is no doubt that the Ignatian retreat is an experience of deep solitude. For thirty days one prays in a structured way about five hours daily, and in the interstices continues the search for God less intensely but no less totally, through every waking moment, including the moments of going to sleep and waking up, about which the text has something to say., Few retreatants will ever again in their lives experience such a deep and sustained solitude.

Still, there is built into the very structure of the experience a daily conversation with a companion of the journey, some wise and sympathetic person who helps from a posture of faith and empathetic detachment. The psychic and spiritual power of this daily communion during a half hour or more is hard to overestimate. It is the power of silence shared, the experience of the solitary encounter with God being extended to reverent dialogue in God's presence with another believer. Though it does not require friendship in any proper sense, it commonly creates a bond between retreatant and director which is one of the signal graces of the retreat. I have heard many directors of the Spiritual Exercises gratefully exclaim how their own faith has been nurtured in these dialogues with the retreatants.

The Ignatian retreat experience, especially as conducted today, also comprises a societal dimension. This is not a question of the director influencing the retreatant to pray about the world's ills; such an effort could well be intrusive into the solitary dialogue of the retreatant with God. In addition, there are other kinds of exercises more apt to heighten the sensibilities of Christians to the plight of the poor, the inequity of political and

economic structures, and the like. A retreatant who has already
been involved in such social exercises will quite naturally be
moved beyond private spiritual concerns during the Ignatian retreat. But the societal dimension of the retreat itself is contained more in the material and human climates within which
prayer takes place. For example, retreatants are most often
away from home, usually far from the noise and bustle of the
city, in a setting of natural beauty. Meals taken together in silence, often to the accompaniment of quiet music, are a societal
setting congruous with prayer and the fostering of dispositions
of deep faith. The daily celebration of the Eucharist, usually in a
contemplative style, adds elements of ritual, symbol, and structure to the shared experience. By its very character, the
Eucharistic celebration situates the members of a retreat group
within the global context of God's people on every continent.
From the rising of the sun to its setting, the "Mass over the
World" (in Teilhard's phrase) is always being celebrated, and
even when it is not made material for reflection it forms a very
real and powerful societal context for every retreat Eucharist.

Those who have been through the long Ignatian retreat have
often remarked in wonder how deep a bond can be created
within a group in which the solitude of each becomes the communion of all with very little verbal communication. It would
seem that deep intimacy with God on the part of individuals
within this special context of faith tends to foster a deeper intimacy among them than do more superficial sharings over a
period of many months or even years.

That such energies should be generated by the Ignatian retreat made together should not surprise us. Our faith is powerfully aided by the witness of other people's faith, and in the solitude of the retreat we are more disposed to be nourished and
inspired by that faith. Ignatius knew nothing, of course, of the
three chairs in the cabin by Walden pond, and in creating the
Spiritual Exercises he may not have been thinking of fifty or
sixty people making them at the same time. But his pragmatic
method, in today's adaptation, is proving to be a major energy
resource for Church and society.

Impact on Communal Ministry

Finally, a brief word about how the Spiritual Exercises can be viewed in relationship to community life and ministry. For community members and ministers singly they can provide a wellspring of life, especially at periods when burnout or discouragement is a threat. But they can do more. As I came to realize in 1976 at Baguio in the Philippines, they can be for Jesuits and others a paradigm of Christian decision and action, communal as well as individual. What the retreat experience, guided by this distinctive method, can do to dispose an individual for basic option, comparable exercises, deliberately chosen and carefully structured, can do for ministerial teams and other kinds of basic communities. The primary point of application is that ministry and community are shaped by decision. A distinctive note of Ignatian spirituality says that life is for transformation through free and discerning choice. The further Ignatian insight that contemplative openness to the movement of grace is the key to holy decision is capable of being structured into group processes which enable ministry teams and communities to arrive in tranquility and freedom at consensus. Hence, the models exhibited in the four previous chapters find a focus in the Ignatian exercises viewed precisely as method, and employed as a paradigm for the communal discernment of spirits — another term for Christian decision.

Questions for Reflection

For personal spirituality:

1. If you have made an Ignatian retreat, especially a 30-day one, to what extent has that experience corresponded to this chapter's description?
2. How sensitive do you feel yourself to be to the importance of physical and societal settings for times of retreat and for your ordinary prayer? What kinds of settings have been helpful for you?
3. In planning future retreats, what kind (directed or preached; with a group or in total solitude) do you think is more likely to meet your present needs and attractions?

For ministry:

1. Has your ministry team ever shared a retreat?
2. Does your service as a team to whatever group you minister to include regular or occasional retreats for deepening the faith life of the people?
3. Are you familiar with "at home retreats," "the Spiritual Exercises in Daily Life," and similar programs for making retreat without disengaging from one's regular routines of home and work?

6

Fidelity: Constancy/Surprise

In the summer of 1968, Woodstock College, the Jesuit seminary where I had taught for fourteen years, was preparing to celebrate the centennial of its foundation in the countryside outside of Baltimore. It was also beginning to plan its move to Morningside Heights in Manhattan, where, after several dramatic years in a difficult milieu, it would close its doors in 1975. In retrospect, the talk which I gave that summer at Woodstock at a workshop on religious formation, in which I dealt with "the crisis of permanency in religious life," appears quite congruous with the special challenges of those turbulent years in the U.S. church and society. In 1969 I gave a modified version of the talk in Sister Formation regional programs in Cincinnati, Chicago, and Denver. The presentation made its way into print in *Sisters Today*.[1] In continuing to brood about the theme of commitment, I wrote another essay on Jesuit commitment as a fraternal covenant for *Studies in the Spirituality of Jesuits* in 1971.[2] It was joined there by an essay by John Haughey which prepared the way for his later popular book, *How Can Anyone Say Forever?* Through the early seventies I continued to give talks on the theme, always trying to develop a more adequate response to the basic question.

At a certain point three symbols appeared in my imagination — the rock, the butterfly, and the ocean waves. They seemed to capture or at least to intimate the paradox of constancy and surprise which I had come to find in the beautiful virtue of fidelity. Both in myself and in my listeners, I felt the special power contained in this symbolic expression of the mystery of fidelity. Many people have written much deeper things about fidelity — I think, for example, about Gabriel Marcel — but because I have never had the occasion to publish anything which contained these three images, the following bit of theological anthropology draws on them to portray a crucial aspect of Christian life and ministry.

Fidelity and Forgiveness

What was described in the late sixties and early seventies as a crisis of permanent commitment for priests and religious was really part of a deeper cultural crisis. The second Vatican Council represented a crucial step in the halting accommodation of the Roman Catholic Church to the culture of modernity. In several of its more significant advances, the Council spoke a Yes to the historical process of secularization, as well as to some of the insights of the Reformers, including Martin Luther's strictures on monastic vows.

The prevailing interpretation of religious vows in the Tridentine Church had been sacralizing in tendency, that is, had spoken a language which accented the discontinuity, not the continuity, of those vows with other human commitments. Even after hereditary monarchs, anointed for life, had given way to elected presidents exercising limited constitutional powers, ecclesiastical structures and mindsets continued to prize the idea of a lifetime of consecration to contemplation or Church office or ministry for priests and religious. The desacralizing tendency in the 20th century Church, which had, for example, already found expression in the switch to the vernacular in liturgy, now manifested itself in widespread doubts about the value and validity of a lifetime commitment for religious. Dealing plausibly with these doubts within a secularized Christian world view required an apologetic for religious vows which would root the theological in the anthropological, and also effectively disengage the perennial power of commitment from its peculiarly medieval garb. Granted that, like the baptismal commitment, this further consecration is a grace-inspired Yes to God, it is still necessary to exhibit its congruity with the basic dynamism of our humanity. Can it be shown that to say Forever is not only compatible with but in some sense mandated by the exigencies of authentic human existence? And what is the language appropriate in a modern and post-modern era for saying "Yes — forever."?

A penetrating observation by Hannah Arendt points, I believe, towards such an anthropological grounding of religious vows. After portraying the human predicament in terms of the irreversibility of the past and the unpredictability of the future, she writes:

> The possible redemption from the predicament of irreversibility — of being unable to undo what has been done, though one did not, or could not, have known what he was doing, is the faculty of forgiving. The remedy for unpredictability, for the chaotic uncertainty of the future, is contained in the faculty to make and keep promises. The two faculties belong together in so far as one of them, forgiving, serves to undo the deeds of the past, whose "sins" hang like Damocles' sword over every new generation; and the other, binding oneself through promise, strives to set up in the ocean of uncertainty, which is the future by definition, islands of security within which not even continuity, let alone durability of any kind, would be possible in the relationships between men.[3]

This linking of fidelity and forgiveness as structural requirements for the future of humankind helps us to counteract a view of religious vows which would see them as necessarily esoteric and alienating. As humanity's future depends on people's willingness to forgive the past, so it depends on their willingness to keep promises and to trust one another for that fidelity. Here, as always, the Word takes flesh in a humanity that needs it and is open to it. Vowed existence, in the radical sense of a persevering will to be faithful, is identical with the call to be human. The question becomes not the one posed in the late sixties, "How can anyone say 'Forever'?" but rather "Can anyone *not* say 'Forever' and still be authentically human?" Not only the Gospel, but the witness of the whole of creation, responds firmly in the negative.

Constancy and Surprise

It is no mere fancy to say that the mystery of being contains within it a certain rhythm which I would designate with the terms "constancy" and "surprise." These are the two poles of a tension which constitutes the dynamic fidelity of being. Take, for example, three manifestations of nature's beauty: the rock, the butterfly, and waves at the seashore. The rock, especially as a mountain, stands for the element of constancy, reliability, "being there," which we look for in faithful friends. Those who are privileged to look out the window each morning at a mountain — the same mountain that was there yesterday and last year and last century — can testify to the assurance, the stability, which is generated by such a gift day after day. And yet — to play a bit with this symbol — the rock is also a microcosm of surprise, indeterminacy, unpredictability. For it to be a rock is contingent on an invisible and never ending dance of the molecules and atoms within. Like every other creature of earth, its being, truth, goodness, and beauty depend on a unique polarity of constancy and surprise, even though its special symbolic role is to manifest and evoke just the constancy.

With the butterfly it is precisely the opposite. Who of us could ever plot the course of one of these lovely creatures across a field of flowers? Unpredictability is the very essence of its place in nature. But this quality depends essentially on its opposite. Without a stable structure — the butterfly's equivalent of a backbone, for example — the delight and surprise which it shows the world would not exist.

The waves at the seashore exercise their mesmerizing power largely because they manifest both constancy and surprise. As we gaze at them, listen to them, and let their ripple or pounding punctuate our own inner ebb and flow, we have absolutely no doubt that this rhythmic breathing of the ocean on the land will continue during the night of our sleep. This is the one sound in the universe which is never silent. In that constancy of the ocean we hear the echo of the eternal fidelity of God, constantly flowing towards us in love. And yet, as we stand and watch successive waves, each one of them uniquely crests and breaks in white foam before dying on the beach. Something holds us to watch the next one, and the next. Watching waves and listening to them is so far from the "see one, see them all" kind of experience which dulls so much of life today — the plastic container, the Howard Johnson orange roof, the detergent commercial, the political or religious platitude. That is why this and similar experiences of nature have the power to heal and restore sensibilities dulled by our culture.

When one moves from such a simple contemplation of the fidelity which is built into nature to the different facets of being human, the same rhythm of fidelity is manifest. It might be studied in detail within the several systems which constitute the physical organism of humans. Psychologically, health and maturity may also be described in these terms. Without constancy in personality and character, a human being must verify Bernard Lonergan's description of "the drifter," or Keniston's sociological profile of "the uncommitted," or even the "nowhere man" of whom the Beatles sang in 1965: "He's a real nowhere man/Sitting in his nowhere land/Making all his nowhere plans for nobody."[4] But it is also true that without an element of surprise and openness to surprise, human personality and character deteriorate to sameness, deadness, dullness.

This same rhythm of constancy and surprise needs to obtain also in families and other groups, if they are to be healthy and generative. The tension and complementarity which we have described between the psychological functions of sensing and intuiting, in individuals, groups, and cultures, may be related to constancy and surprise as constitutive of fidelity. Sensing types tend to be strong on constancy but less able to handle unforeseen situations. Intuiting types sometimes show a certain unreliability, the reverse side of being more ready to adjust to surprise.

Such reflections as these are no more than random indications of an important anthropological truth. Prior to any specifically Christian argument for the value of vowing one's life, the human vocation in all its aspects contains a radical call to a fidelity that is constituted by the union of firmness and open-

ness, constancy and surprise. Commitment is a call to both continuity and discontinuity, a readiness to stand by one's pledged
word but also a willingness to let one's expectations be touched
and challenged by the flow of life. In the hermeneutical circle between the Gospel and an authentic engagement in life, such a
model sends the Christian back to the Gospel to see just how the
rhythm of constancy and surprise occurs there.

God's Fidelity and Surprises

It manifests itself, first, in what the Scriptures have to say
about God. "God is faithful, by whom you have been called to the
communion [the *koinonia*] of his Son, Jesus Christ" (1 Corinthians 1:9). Paul's declaration of the divine fidelity may serve as
a keynote of this reflection on Christian vowing. God who calls
us to vow our existence is God who has both fulfilled the promise
of sending Son and Spirit and, in and through that fulfillment,
pledged once again and with an absolute irrevocability to be
forever Emmanuel, God with us.

There is nothing very new in saying that God is faithful. But
understanding this fidelity according to the paradigm of constancy and surprise invites us to a deeper understanding of how
God is faithful. That God is rock and mountain for the people is
an accustomed and consoling doctrine. But that God is a God of
surprise is itself surprising language. Yet Scripture testifies
how, again and again, in the very fulfillment of his word, in
being the constant one, God acts beyond our expectations and
even against them, calling us to accept, and even to expect, the
unexpected from his hand. Was this not precisely the scandal of
the way in which God sent the Messiah, not in power but in
weakness?

Both in the preaching of Jesus, particularly in the Synoptics,
and in Paul, the test of faith/fidelity is trust, openness to a divine
action that cannot be controlled or predicted beyond the basic
assumption that the One who has promised will be faithful and
loving. God is a butterfly, forever baffling our determined efforts
to capture him in our net and catalogue him along with other
species. He cannot cease to be "God with us." As a friend wrote

after reading through this chapter, "He can't go out to lunch and be God *not* with us." But the *how* of that presence is for God alone to determine.

There is an even more radical question about God's fidelity, which I will mention here without exploring. Does God himself have to live in trust? Is our God the God of surprise only in the sense that he calls *us* to be open to surprise or can he himself be surprised? There is no doubt that Jesus himself registered wonder and surprise, especially when he encountered remarkable faith in simple people. But what of God as God? How, we might wonder, can he be model of our fidelity as it contains such openness unless he too has had experience of the unpredictable, the uncontrollable? Process philosophers and theologians may come more readily to the notion of the divine "surpriseability" than I can do. But even within traditional Thomism some have tried, while affirming God's all wise and powerful providence, to allow for surprise. In any case, the faithful God who made us in his image and invites us to radical trust and openness toward himself, must somehow contain, in a manner infinitely beyond our ken, the fullness of that openness.

Whatever may be said about the divine "surpriseability," there is another perspective — a trinitarian one — from which we may grasp God's fidelity as a unity of constancy and surprise. The eternal Word, made flesh in the person of Jesus Christ, stands for the divine constancy, the once-for-all-pledge, the firm commitment of God to humankind. This is the rock of our faith, and it corresponds to the character of the pledged human word, the promise made once-for-all and never to be broken. John of the Cross' classic statement reminds us that those who look for some new revelation beyond the one already given are asking God to repeat the unrepeatable promise made in giving us his Son who is his Word. Having spoken that Word of promise, God has nothing more to say to us, and we have no need of any further promise. In Jesus we behold God's call to us to stand by every vow we utter to God and to one another. "The Lord has sworn, and will not change his mind" (Psalm 110:4).

If the Word is God's fidelity as constancy, the Spirit is God's

fidelity as surprise. The human word, as fixed sound, as sylla-
ble, as stable vehicle of meaning, is fixed, firm, unchanging. But
the human breath (as well as wind and fire, other symbols of the
Spirit) has the quality of being intangible, amorphous, unde-
fined. The wind blows where it will, and no one knows where it
comes from or whither it goes (John 3:8). As God's Word roots us
in the primordial past, the irrevocable promise, so God's Spirit
opens us to the absolute future which is God, always beyond our
grasp. The unity of Word and Spirit within the godhead, as ema-
nations of the one God, expresses the unity of the constancy and
surprise which constitutes God's fidelity, and ours. When Christians are faithful to their vows, they mirror and participate in
the trinitarian life of God.

In the life and ministry of Jesus we witness this kind of fidelity in its most perfect human embodiment. We see firmness,
obedience, his stern demand on himself and others to live from
the Father's truth. As Paul says, Jesus Christ was not now Yes
and now No — only Yes was in him, so that the Amen which
arises through him from the Christian community goes un-
swervingly to the Father in the Spirit (2 Corinthians 1:19-20).
On the other hand, Jesus' fidelity contained a beautiful openness to surprise. There are hints, especially in the Synoptics, of
an almost childlike wonder and delight at what the Father is
doing beyond the expectations of the Son by bestowing such remarkable faith on ordinary people. Especially if one accepts
what recent Christology has said regarding the very human and
limited character of Jesus' knowledge, his experience of life appears not as a totally assured control by knowledge of his own
destiny, but as a profound learning experience. In that likeness
to us of which the letter to the Hebrews speaks, Jesus too had to
engage in the risk of walking without knowing what was ahead
of him on the road (Hebrews 5:9). Only so could he model for us
a fidelity compounded of both constancy and surprise.

Fidelity and the Church
What eventually emerges from this line of reflection is an
overall view of salvation history as covenant, that is, as the en-

gagement of the God of constancy and surprise with the whole of humankind through Jesus Christ. When the reflection moves from Christology to ecclesiology, the same characteristics of vowed existence are seen in every aspect of the Church's life. A detailed treatment of all these aspects is beyond our intention here. Let us rather present a few headlines which readers may wish to amplify.

First, the relationship of Christ and the Church is one of mutual fidelity and, we have to add, of recurring infidelity on the part of a Church still on pilgrimage. Paul's use of special spousal imagery in Ephesians chapter 5, together with the symbolism of the marriage feast of the Lamb and the Bride in the book of Revelation, provide a New Testament base for reflecting on this vowed relationship. From the perspective of the constancy/surprise model, specific ecclesiological doctrines, structures, and practices have a new light shed on them. When the charism represented by the language of infallibility is considered, for example, can we not say that it tilts our understanding of the Church as faithful teacher decidedly to the side of constancy in order to provide assurance and security to Christian believers? And might the traditional Protestant reluctance to accept this language not be interpreted as a desire to honor the element of surprise which must always be a part of an authentic posture of faith and fidelity on the part of a Church that is both sinful and holy?

Second, among various ecclesiologies which have historically complemented and clashed with one another, a broad typology of Word and Spirit ecclesiologies might be applicable. The dyad of institution/event would correspond to the constancy/surprise and Word/Spirit dyads.

Third, while a sound theological understanding of the distinction between charism and institution requires respect for complexity — as for example in the recognition that in the Church office and institution are charismatic — our dyad might find a specific application in situating religious life within the institutional Church. If these and other grassroots or charismatic communities are to make their distinctive contribution, they must

not be absorbed into the hierarchical structure so as to be, in this
sense, clericalized. Vatican II's Constitution on the Church cau-
tions against such an absorption, and the new law of the
Church, in principle at least, makes much of the autonomy of
religious communities. But one gets the impression that some
Church officials want to leave nothing to surprise, and are anxious to reduce as far as possible any tensions which might en-
danger the total and instant harmony among different elements
in the Church. Such attitudes are, in my opinion, a grave risk to
the free flow of ecclesial energies from the grassroots of the
Church, where the Spirit is continually providing that the
Church's constancy not degenerate into stagnancy.

Fourth, it goes without saying that our model provides a base
for reflecting on *all* vows of Christians, beginning with those of
baptism and including those of marriage, religious life, and commitment to sacred office. Given past emphases on constancy, at
least in the Roman Catholic tradition, I would suggest that reflection on each of these kinds of promises would do well to tilt
the balance somewhat in favor of surprise, the unpredictable
movement of the Spirit, and the necessity for every Christian vocation to be open to what is new. The term "permanent" as
applied to Christian commitment has unfortunate connotations, as it seems to invite a purely temporal understanding of
what is being vowed. What counts, of course, is the quality of the
promising, and of the fulfilling. Whether it is a question of baptism, marriage, religious profession, or ordination to office,
what is being pledged is a serious commitment to deepen one's
participation in the paschal mystery, God's own solemn covenant with humankind in Christ, within some specified area of the
Church's life.

Fifth, in each instance of Christian vowing, the partner in covenant is both God and the Christian community which
mediates our relationship with God. Covenant and mutual fidelity to covenant is, in Gospel perspective, a dimension of the law
of love, and, as Karl Rahner has shown in a new way, love of God
and love of neighbor are inextricably interwoven. Whatever may
be said about so-called private vows, the act of public vowing in

the Church entails fidelity both to God and to the Church. In this connection, there is an interesting contrast in the formulation of marriage and religious vows. In the former, what is accented is the vow to the human partner — "I take *you* for better or for worse . . . " In the latter, the accent is on the sacred promise to God. In both cases, however, there is a mediation through which the beloved neighbor whom we do see represents the mysterious God whom we cannot see. And this representation takes place in both directions, so to speak, with respect to the one who vows. The one who risks plunging more deeply into the paschal mystery through baptism or some subsequent commitment is both pledging fidelity to God through fidelity to the ecclesial community, and is in turn receiving the pledge of God's fidelity through the pledged fidelity of the community. Given the fallibility of every commitment coming from our sinful humanity, there is a poignancy as well as a boldness inherent in every instance of Christian vowing. Only a faith that is open to surprise makes it possible to commit ourselves to the One whose trustworthiness is absolute, through the mediation of human beings as fragile and fallible as ourselves.

Sixth, it follows from this mediation of the divine through the human that Christian covenant is always more than a mere human contract. As Church ministries have become more professional, they have called for formal contracts binding in civil law, specifying the rights and obligations of the parties to the contract. This is a healthy development, especially in providing a greater societal assurance that the basic human and Christian rights of all who live and labor within Church structures will be respected. Still, when such employment takes on the character of Christian ministry, there is no ecclesiastical contract which is not at the same time an ecclesial covenant, participating in the fidelity of Christ and the Church. How the exigencies of secular justice and Christian covenant are simultaneously to be honored is often, in the concrete, difficult to discern. What will be said in Chapter 9 about love and justice will bear some relationship to this problem.

Crises of Fidelity

All that has been said thus far may be helpful for dealing with both spiritual and pastoral challenges in which fidelity is at stake. Major examples in today's Church are found in the all too common occurrence of crisis in vocations to marriage, religious life, or ecclesiastical office. In each case a baptized and confirmed Christian has spoken a deep and specific Yes, has said "Forever," to God and to other human beings. This commitment, through its mutuality, has said to these others that in living out their own covenants they can rely on the one now vowing to be faithful to his or her own vows. But now the stress and change inherent in all human journeys has brought the person to a moment of radical questioning of what has been undertaken. Only those who have experienced such moments of crisis, in their own commitment or in others whom they have tried to help, can fully appreciate the difficulty. Here are some basic guidelines which emerge from the approach to fidelity taken in this chapter.

First, the personal covenant of each person with God, the call to constancy and surprise written into one's human vocation, is the anchor and rock for anyone who enters upon a crisis of commitment with a need to discern one's future way. Polonius' ". . . to thine own self be true . . . " states the inescapable responsibility of each person created in God's image to be faithful to a unique call that has been inscribed in one's very being.

Second, for Christians this personal covenant with God finds ecclesial expression in baptism and confirmation, to which all subsequent ecclesial vowings must be referred as to a normative base. When more specific commitments are called into question, recourse to the baptismal covenant can preserve both firmness and clarity as we try to be fully faithful.

Third, as there is no covenant with God which is not, in some fashion, a covenant with other human beings, the discerning reappraisal of a particular ecclesial commitment must not take place in isolation. When I became a Jesuit, for example, I shared with those who represented the Society of Jesus the discernment of my apparent call to share my life with this ecclesial community. In the subsequent four decades or so, it could well have happened — though in fact it did not — that the God of surprise should raise for me a question of following my human and baptismal call in another context. In the discerning of such a possibility, one basic criterion of authenticity is whether I am willing to share the discernment with one or another person who, in whatever fashion, represents the community which has taken the risk of sharing this special covenant with me.

Relationship to Earlier Models

After all these reflections on fidelity, one might ask whether it makes that much difference whether our lives, relationships, and structures in the Church continue to make room for the language of vowed existence. Do we really need the language of saying "Forever" in proclaiming the Good News to future generations? For me there is no question but that we do. Why this is so may be expressed through the theme which links the various chapters of this book — energy and power. From both anthropological and theological points of view vowing adds to human life, even beyond the contribution of firm willing and clear social declaration of serious intent, enormous energies which are not otherwise available for our life together on this planet. Hannah Arendt's analysis expresses this contribution with cogency. Without radical trust among humans, humankind has no future. When the founders of our American democracy wrote, as they shared the risks of revolution, "We mutually pledge to each other our lives, our fortunes, our sacred honor," powerful energies flowed among them and beyond them, deepening and confirming the bonds which already united them. The same is true of all the great and little covenants of history, to the degree to which they transcend merely functional contracts. The confluence of constancy and surprise, firmness and openness, determination and vulnerability, and the distinctive mutuality which results from this confluence, is a gift that humankind can never do without.

These energies flow from solitude, friendship, and society. It is important that vowing, like all the basic constituents of the human endeavor, be regarded integrally, as suggested by the

Walden model. Vowing is simultaneously a commitment to personal authenticity, a special engagement in intimacy, and an act that is profoundly political. My vows as a Christian or a Jesuit or a priest are indeed an instance of the unique self-creation in God's image to which we are fully empowered by the gift of the Spirit. Those vows both express and confirm a self-definition present at the very core of existence, and so have the "I can do no other" quality of Luther's beautiful statement. Just as a unique person, therefore, I have rich energies available to me from the specific ways I have identified myself by a commitment to constancy and surprise.

At the same time all vowing is deeply interpersonal, not only with respect to God but with respect to one or more persons with whom I have thrown in my lot, and who have taken the corresponding risk with me. I have already commented on how this human mutuality mediates my covenant with God. This adds still more energy to my struggle to be faithful. Anyone who is a radical bachelor (not to be confused with following the vocation of the single life — there are married bachelors) is deprived of a great deal of the power that comes from this interpersonal aspect of covenant fidelity.

All vowing is likewise societal or political, in the sense that our vowing modifies the public climates in which we humans pursue our goals and shape our destiny. As with other versions of societal energy, vowing makes a public difference beyond our reflecting about it and speaking of it. It affects the very air we breathe. I personally would like to hear church bells ring for every baptism, every wedding, every ordination, every religious profession, to signalize that the life of the whole Church and of the surrounding society is no longer the same as it was a few hours ago. The dynamic of forgiveness and fidelity analyzed by Hannah Arendt is the specific form of energy that flows from vows into political trust and public hope. Because of vows made and kept, nothing is absolutely irreversible in history, and the unpredictablity of the future ceases to induce chaos into the present. When one considers the radical mistrust and radical despair which erodes every effort to bring about a peaceful and just global society, one is led to prize every instance, religious or not, Christian or not, where people pledge themselves to be faithful and take pains to carry out their pledges.

Functions in Fidelity

We have already made some brief observations on how vowing relates to our previous reflection on the Jungian typology. We would add here that viewing fidelity as a dynamic of constancy and surprise is congruous with the experience we have of the contrast of perceiving and judging. The language which accents constancy in the fulfillment of commitments is generally congruous with a preference for judging over perceiving. "I made my vows, I knew what I was doing, I have assumed certain responsibilities, and I cannot turn back," is a statement which fits those persons, and that aspect of personality in all of us which comes quickly to judgment and decision. When, however, we hear "I need to renew my commitment every day," or "How can I be sure that God's Spirit will be moving in me the same way ten years from now?", we hear an echo of the tendency to favor a perceiving posture towards life, to be ready for the surprises which may come. Both kinds of language are legitimate, and each of the two accents is open to its own temptation toward infidelity. In the one case, the constancy of a mummy, and in the other, the rootlessness of a dead leaf blown about at the whimsy of the wind, point to the loss of the dynamic tension without which genuine fidelity is lost.

There seems little need at this point to offer more specific spiritual or ministerial suggestions on the promotion of human and Christian fidelity. The following questions will help both individuals and ministerial teams to reflect on how they can profit from the considerations of this chapter.

Questions for Reflection

For personal spirituality:

1. Does the model of fidelity as a blend of constancy and sur-

    prise help you to understand your own vows and other commitments?

2. Do you find yourself more inclined to speak the language of constancy or of surprise?
3. At this point in your life, which of the two seems to need accenting?

For ministry:

1. Among the individuals, families, and other groups which you serve, what cultural attitudes do you find regarding fidelity? How do these affect the mentality and practice of people from the standpoint of the Gospel?
2. In preaching, catechesis, and other vehicles of ministry, what kind of language do you think is needed in your particular milieu, and in our culture in general? What images, metaphors, stories are especially attractive with respect to such evangelization?

7
Providence/Prudence

This chapter has not exactly been an afterthought. But through the first draft of this book I somehow had fused the creator/creature and providence/prudence model, which I shall be discussing here, with the development/liberation model of the following chapter. In the process of revision I came to see that the two themes, while intimately related, needed separate treatment, and had in fact a different origin in my personal history.

The pre-history of my musings about the theme of creation dates back to about 1940, when, prior to my becoming a Jesuit, I came across Frederick William Faber's devout *Creature and Creator*, along with a powerful orchestration of St. Ignatius' Principle and Foundation in Louis Lallement's austere classic, *Spiritual Doctrine*. Both of these works fed into the Lacouture paradigm of spiritual perfection which, as I have narrated in Chapter 5, turned my life in a new direction during my recuperation from tuberculosis. Throughout my years of Jesuit training I breathed deeply from a spiritual atmosphere which cultivated a sense of radical and total dependency on God the creator. Year after year, the directors of our eight-day annual retreat would wax eloquent on the basis of the inexorable logic of the Principle and Foundation.

In addition, my philosophical and theological studies, heavily scholastic in character, introduced me to the various pre-modern controversies — on divine omnipotence and human freedom, on divine providence, human freedom and evil, and on grace and freedom — all of which were distinct ways of coming at the same basic mystery and problem of who God is for us and who we are for God. As a Jesuit scholastic faithfully echoing the

accepted "Molinist" formulations, and viewing the opposed
"Bannezian" positions as sinister aberrations, I lived and moved
in an ambience that knew little or nothing of the scandal that
these traditional teachings represented for modern thought.

Two authors, a Dominican and a Jesuit, brought me in the fifties to an experience of liberation from the hardened categories
of the now antiquated *de auxiliis* disputes. The Dominican was
Antonin Sertillanges, whose little book, *L'Idee de Création dans
la Philosophie de Saint Thomas d'Aquin*, stripped away, in what
has been called "an agnosticism of definition," the anthropomor-
phizing "signs of reason," the detailed divine game plan, so to
speak. Through such constructs later scholastics had departed
from Aquinas' willingness to let God be God in philosophical and
theological discourse. I was subsequently elated when a respected Jesuit teacher in Rome, Guy de Broglie, drew on Sertillanges for his reflections on providence and grace.

When I began to teach Christology back at Woodstock in 1954,
my liberation was completed by a powerful paragraph of Karl
Rahner, which presented the creator/creature relationship
dialectically so as to make God's freedom the source and not the
limit of human freedom. I can think of no single paragraph in
my theological reading which has been more consciously in my
mind in approaching the mystery of our relationship with God
and with one another. Further confirmation came from conversations with a brilliant Jesuit humanist, William Lynch, whose
Images of Hope challenged me to accept the full implications of
the more abstract views of Sertillanges and Rahner. As my reflections will disclose, I was also stimulated by some challenging
statements of Dietrich Bonhoeffer and John Milhaven.

As I will indicate below, the creator/creature relationship and
the providence/prudence relationship are at heart one mystery and form one problem, seen from different perspectives.
Through writers like Jacques Maritain and Josef Pieper I had
been introduced to the remarkable choreographing of all the virtues, including prudence, to be found in Aquinas' *Summa
Theologica*. In fact, even before I became a Jesuit, the *Catholic*

Worker, in disseminating Eric Gill's ideas on art as good work, had acquainted me with the distinction between art as *recta ratio factibilium* and prudence as *recta ratio agibilium*, dealing respectively with the beautiful (or ugly) *products* of human behavior and the *self-transformation* (or self-diminishment) wrought by that same behavior. Later, in the fifties, a chapter of Henri de Lubac's book, *The Drama of Atheistic Humanism*, which dealt with the strictures of Proudhon against the Christian teaching on divine providence, helped me to see the repugnance of modern thinkers for this doctrine. Finally, reading Jean de Caussade's spiritual classic, *Abandonment to Divine Providence*, helped me to situate the theological question within a spiritual perspective.

When I came to develop a course at Woodstock on providence and grace, it was this relationship of human prudence and divine providence which fascinated me. I look back nostalgically at an aborted publication stemming from that interest. During Vatican II Gus Weigel was negotiator for several articles in the theological encyclopedia, *Sacramentum Mundi*, to be published in German, English, and other languages. Gus offered me the article on providence, and I undertook a very synthetic treatment which centered on human prudence as sacrament of divine providence. I was rather happy with the result, which I sent off to the editor. A few years later, much to my surprise, the encyclopedia appeared with an article on providence by a Continental theologian. Apparently my precious creation had disappeared, without a word from the editor, somewhere in the bowels of this great enterprise. Somehow, I felt, divine providence was involved.

Creation and Freedom

There is a sense in which the Christian doctrine of creation pervades all other doctrines, including Christology and soteriology. True, in the special salvation history which is the story of the Old Testament, God was experienced as savior prior to being experienced as creator. Still, every credal utterance carries an implicit assumption about the radical relationship of the universe to the One who made it "out of nothing" (*ex nihilo*).

All too often our understanding of God as creator succumbs to
the perennial temptation to anthropomorphism; we forget that
the inevitable shaping of our concepts of God to the limits of
human understanding calls for a continual overcoming of each
positive statement with a disclaimer of any direct knowledge of
divinity. Anthropomorphism as a theological vice consists not in
the inescapable finitude of our concepts but in a certain lack of
vigilance against projecting this finitude on to God through
judgments made outside of the circle of mystery. When such
ideological irreverence becomes translated into the "religious"
behavior of people like ourselves who convey to others that God
is our personal possession, these others are often scandalized
into an agnostic or atheistic response to our "witness." This is
true especially when God is represented in thought and action
as an absolute monarch providing security for his subjects at the
price of their human dignity. It also happens when God's power
and providence are made an excuse for passive resignation in
the face of evil, especially the evil resulting from injustice.

The rejection of theism by the mainstream of modern thought
is in large part the result of such a disfigurement of belief in the
lives of Christians. Sartre's "If I am, God is not; if God is, I am
not," and the older charges of thinkers like Marx and Proudhon
that Christianity has incapacitated its adherents for shaping
history, reminds us of our terrible power to hide the face of God.
However unpalatable Sartre's saying may be, it is not a sheer
caricature of traditional religious understanding and social behavior. On the contrary, the common devout view would have it
that because God is creator, I must accept limitations on my
freedom. Sin then becomes basically a Promethean overreach-
ing of creaturely limitations, and our primary duty as creatures
is conceived as subjection to a God modelled on the absolute
monarchs of certain periods of history. Such a conceptualization
makes Christian doctrine vulnerable to the critique of a culture
which, at least in its profession, prizes nothing more than freedom and the spirit of adventure. To such eyes God appears as a
puppeteer, skillfully manipulating the strings through which

every movement of God's creatures is controlled. Especially when such a theoretical image of our God is interwoven with submission to political tyranny or acquiescence in economic injustice, the real face of God is distorted in the eyes of those who do not believe.

There is more than one theoretical way of correcting the distortion. Here I shall sketch out the views of some thinkers who have helped me at various stages.

Though it might seem that neo-Thomism has run its course, we can still learn from its more eminent exponents. Sertillanges' contribution was to strip away the accumulated barnacles of several centuries. Like Aquinas, he was content to say very little about "the One whom we call God," and he insisted that what we can and must say not be taken as a definition. Augustine's *"Si comprehendisti, non est Deus"* (if you have totally grasped God, it is not God you are grasping) epitomizes Sertillanges' austere understanding of God as creator. Dealing with the classic conundrum of reconciling divine power with human freedom, he simply refused to play the famous game of assigning to God a multiplicity of calculating choices made in "metaphysical moments" prior to or consequent upon the divine foreknowledge of possible or "futurible" human choices. The only real order in creation is not in God but in what God has created. That cosmic order, from galaxies to the dance of protons and electrons, is an order radically caused by God, who is both infinitely beyond it and infinitely within it; *therefore* (not "nevertheless") it is an order which is radically free to be its own immanent self with all its dynamism and complexity.

At the risk of baffling some readers, let me set down, untranslated, an aphorism of Aquinas which for me is almost poetry. It expresses the truth that the succession and complexity of divine order are not in God's inner being but in the creation which it guides. *"Vult ergo deus hoc esse propter hoc, sed non propter hoc vult hoc."*[1] In paraphrase: God wills that a relationship of order obtain between distinct created realities, but his willing of one created reality does not cause him to will another created reality."

I must acknowledge that this Thomistic view of God, based on the Aristotelian metaphysics of potency and act in which God appears as *actus purus*, has its vulnerabilities. Neo-Thomists struggle with the apparent implication that, while we are really related to God, God is not really related to us. Such is the risk of any philosophy which so accents the divine transcendence. The value of Sertillanges' interpretation is that it calls us to a deep reverence in the presence of incomprehensible mystery.

Our Freedom Shows God's Will

Karl Rahner, speaking more like Hegel than like Aquinas, accents even more the element of paradox and dialectic contained in the mystery.[2] Creaturely autonomy exists not in spite of but precisely because of the creature's radical dependence on the creator. In human creatures, made in God's own image, this translates into a freedom at once radically dependent and radically unfettered, even, as Rahner insists, with respect to God. Only God, no one else, and precisely as God, is able to constitute another freedom simultaneously in a radical dependence on himself, and *therefore* (not "nevertheless") in radical self-possession and freedom. The traditional prayer of the liturgy epitomizes this philosophical thesis in a political metaphor, ". . . *cui servire regnare est* . . . " (to be your slave is to be a monarch). Radical obedience to God is the quintessence of human self-possession.

Dietrick Bonhoeffer's *Letters and Papers from Prison* offer a more existential expression of the same message.[3] Struggling with the challenge posed by the historical secularization of the West, this noble captive risked a language that itself appeared secularistic. "God is teaching us that we must live as men who can get along very well without him . . . Before God and with him we live without God."

It is this last phrase which especially signals the affinity of Bonhoeffer's views with those of Sertillanges and Rahner. We are to look for no divine intervention in history. God has no other point of entry into the human struggle than our human freedom.

While Christianity — and Bonhoeffer – are far from accepting the basic premise of secularism (the irrelevancy of Christian faith to the historic human endeavor), it can, in order to learn from the heresy of secularism and to enter into the viewpoint of modernity, divest itself of the security blanket contained in traditional notions of creation and providence. However risky Bonhoeffer's formulations may be, they have the power to serve as a cathartic, cleansing these doctrines of faith, and the attitudes which they foster, of sluggishness and languor.

William Lynch deals perceptively with the hauntedness which often afflicts religious persons as in effect they make God's will to be a reified command "out there," — and God help me if I don't find it. God really doesn't care, says Lynch, whether I choose coffee or tea. God's delight is that I choose.[4] Though this treatment of the classic tension between divine and human freedom offers no metaphysical resolution, it can serve as a practical assurance or challenge for the overly anxious or overly dependent believer.

John Milhaven, in a popular article published in the midst of the student revolts of the late sixties, put the same basic message quite provocatively; increasingly through the years his language has appeared to me, after the first shock, as both solid and deep. He entitled his article, "Be like me — be free."[5] He was saying to the rebellious students of that period, "Do what you really want to do. Exercise your freedom to the full." The article angered some of Milhaven's colleagues, especially among Jesuits. And I must confess that at first I considered it rather one-sided. But now I would endorse it wholeheartedly, and paraphrase it somewhat as follows: God, who always does what he wants, has made us in his image, and wants our exercise of freedom to reflect his. Doing always what we really want might seem at first to be a hedonistic formula. In a Pauline and Augustinian understanding of freedom, however, it is really equivalent to Jesus' saying of himself, "I do always what pleases him" and "My food is to do the will of the one who sent me" (John 8:29; 4:34). When we are really ourselves, when our behavior proceeds not from compulsive, neurotic forces working from within

or from the surrounding culture but from our own core of freedom and dignity, it will be because we are attuned to God's
Spirit enlightening and inviting us to be our real selves. Thus
the transcendence of God accented by Sertillanges and Rahner,
and in a different way by Lynch, is here understood only together with the (trinitarian) immanence of God who, as Holy
Spirit, is the deepest reality within the creation, enabling and
ennobling the full exercise of our freedom. Doing always what
we want to do is, therefore, the quintessence of Christian obedience.

We see this in Jesus himself. His looking always to the Father
for the direction of his life in no way limited his self-possession
and freedom.[6] "No one takes my life from me," he said, "I lay it
down of my own free will and, as it is in my power to lay it down,
so it is in my power to take it up again" (John 10:1). This consciousness of unfettered freedom on the part of the all-holy Son
of God contrasts strongly with the state of radical sinfulness described by Paul: "I find myself not doing what I want to do, and
doing what I don't want to do" (Romans 7:15). It is the sinner
who doesn't do what he or she really wants. It is the saints who
have grown to the condition of doing what they want, and want-
ing what they do.

Providence in Prudence

Thus far in this chapter we have been considering the mystery
of our relationship to God in the language of creator/creature
and, derivatively, divine freedom/human freedom. The dyad
providence/prudence offers another way of coming at the same
paradox. The source of the model for theological reflection on
this theme is our capacity and need to plan and execute various
schemas, from finding the right movie on a rainy Sunday to
making a choice of one's vocation in life. In a Thomistic analysis,
divine providence is to human prudence as the divine idea(s) are
to human wisdom. The latter pair has to do with creative process
viewed absolutely; the former has to do precisely with *order* or
the complexus of relationships involved in planning and execut-

ing some creative dream. Also, as I have already indicated, prudence is contrasted by Aquinas with art; the quality of art is to be judged by the product (arti-*fact*), whereas the quality of prudence is to be found in the human action itself, especially in its transformation (or deformation) of the human agent. And, like providence, the virtue of prudence — whose complexities Aquinas explores in the language of different "parts" — lies in the capacity for skilful ordering of many elements towards a harmonious fulfillment of purpose and manifestation of meaning.

There would be no great value in repeating for the providence/ prudence dyad the same treatment we have given to the creator/ creature dyad. Instead, let me briefly suggest that the relationship of human prudence and divine providence can be enlightened by recourse to the basic notion of *sacrament*, and expressed in the statement that human prudence is the primary sacrament of divine providence. The familiar catechism definition of sacraments as "outward signs instituted by Christ to give grace" crystallizes a traditional analysis in which the notions of instrument and sign are the toys for theological play. Sacraments effect by signifying. They are basically tools of communication. They *do* by *saying*. If we want to know what God and the Christian community are doing in a particular sacrament, we consider the symbolic gesture: pouring water, anointing with oil, offering and sharing bread and wine, etc. Similarly, the primary place to look in order to experience that divine wisdom "deploys her strength from one end of the earth to the other, ordering all things for good" (Wisdom 8:1) is not the harmony of the subrational creation, but rather the way in which human beings plan and execute their various schemes. To take one of the most striking exercises of ecclesial prudence in recent centuries: when good Pope John XXIII threw open that window and let fresh currents of the Spirit flow into all the rooms and corridors of the Vatican and the universal Church, he was launching a great and complex act of human prudence which, in its positive impact, has symbolized for us the loving wisdom of God in guiding the Church and the whole of humankind in our era.

Other Models and Prudence

Before musing on some of the spiritual and pastoral implications of this model, it may be well briefly to link it with the themes of some of the preceding chapters, by way of hints which readers might like to pursue. Sacraments are channels of divine power and energy within the total ecclesial and human world. To the degree to which the spiritual and pastoral task is, as our first chapter has suggested, to disclose and set free the energies contained within the human, the present consideration indicates how, by its sacramental power, human prudence can make rich energies available for our personal growth and for our various ministries.

The Walden model of Chapter 2 can likewise be joined to the providence/prudence perspective, and then we recognize that this sacrament of Christian decision is at once intrapersonal, interpersonal, and societal in its nature. One could, for example, analyze what went into the great decisions of Vatican II from key persons, from their close collaboration, and from the structuring of the conciliar processes toward the final documents.

There is also the possibility of engaging in an analysis of human prudence — and hence of divine providence — which highlights the contribution of each of the four facets of personality described in Chapter 3. Correlating those functions with the various "parts" of prudence described by Aquinas could be a fascinating game: care to attend to the facts: *sensing;* the capacity to envision various alternatives and contingencies, benign or malevolent: *intuiting*; sensitivity to "reasons of the heart" within the decisional process: *feeling*; and the overarching skill of bringing the various stages and elements of a complex decisional process together in some basic order: *thinking.*

Chapters 4 and 5, dealing with the rhythm of action/contemplation in general and then with a similar rhythm in the Ignatian Exercises, have their theological underpinnings in doctrine of the creation and providence. For example, there is famous dictum, attributed to Ignatius, about the appropriate attitudes for prayer and action. Actually, two forms of the axiom have come down to us. The one which is more likely authentic is dialectical in character: Pray as if everything depends on *you*; then act as if everything depends on God. In this form the axiom is saying: Pray with a sense of your urgent need of grace if your action is to be holy; act with trust that God's grace will suffice in the face of your own limitations. In its non-dialectical form the axiom goes: pray as if everything depends on God, then act as if everything depends on you. Both forms seek to deal with the grace/freedom or providence/prudence mystery in a balanced fashion. The more dialectical form has the advantage of warning us against conceiving of prayer as a request that God substitute for our lack of prudence and courage, and against conceiving of action as an autonomous endeavor in which God, having provided free will, now becomes a mere interested onlooker. Like all the models of this book, these formulas are just formulas, and they always fall short of expressing the mystery. But having recourse to them from time to time can be supportive of our lived engagement in the mystery.

Finally, the present chapter can help us to appreciate more deeply the dialectic of fidelity described in the previous chapter. Our constancy finds support as we appreciate that it *does* depend on our human exertions, but also from our realization that the power of God's providence, while not substituting for our exertions, can make our efforts fruitful beyond our expectations. Knowing that God is guiding the course of our personal and shared history helps us to be open to the unexpected results of our action. A dialectical reading of Philippians 2:12-13 crystallizes the insight we have been playing with: we are to exert ourselves towards our final salvation precisely *because* God is exerting himself within us. And, says Paul, the appropriate attitude towards this agonic interplay of divine and human prudence is "awe and wonder" (as one version of the literal "fear and trembling" would have it).

Spiritual and Pastoral Practice

How can this understanding of what it means to be a creature of God, and of what it means for God's providence to be guiding our prudent struggle to be faithful, make a difference for our spiritual growth? It can surely help us to understand God and our relationship to God if, from time to time we ponder these basic doctrines of our faith, especially with the help of Scriptures. More specifically, and practically, I would suggest that sometimes, in our "consciousness examen," we seek to be in touch with our affectivity with respect to the movements of anxiety and trust, sloth and zeal. More pointedly, we can occasionally ask ourselves to what degree trust and zeal are alternative postures, or to what extent we have come to taste a little what is habitual in the great saints: an integration of trust and zeal, complacency and concern (see Chapter 5), both in the ordinary experience of every day and in moments of special crisis.

Pastorally the theme of the present chapter takes us back to the critique addressed to Christianity by some of the modern philosophers. "Social quietism" is a common name for the radically slothful temptation of many Christians to shrug piously in the face of the world's injustice while mumbling devoutly about divine providence making all things work out for good. "Social activism" in a radical doctrinal sense is the opposite distortion, a concrete unreadiness to put ourselves, especially our freedom, into God's hands, not to substitute for it by his divine freedom, but to let him guide and transform it towards a consuming zeal that is also a consummate trust.

Questions for Reflection

For personal spirituality:

1. Does the Christian doctrine of *creation* provide me with any special light and nourishment in my spiritual journey?
2. Is *prudence* a positive or negative term for me, and have I experienced in my life any tension between taking responsibility for my life and trusting in God's *providence*?

For ministry:

1. To what extent, if any, are the individuals and groups to

whom you minister vulnerable to the charge of either social quietism of social activism?

2. How, concretely, does your team so minister as to make it manifest that all depends ultimately on God?

8

Development/Liberation

Two speaking engagements, in Washington D.C. about 1970 and in the Philippines in 1971, represent in retrospect a significant shift in my reflection towards more immediate concern with Third World perspectives. This is far from saying that I only then began to be interested in social justice. As a student at Xavier High School in 1935, I had interviewed Dorothy Day for our school magazine; and at my graduation from St. Peter's College in 1941 (the fiftieth anniversary of Leo XIII's Encyclical on the condition of the working class, and the tenth anniversary of Pius XI's Encyclical on the reconstruction of the social order), I had given the salutatory talk on Leo XIII (commencements were different in those days). Largely because my parents were Irish immigrants and because my father was, until his death at 95, a member of a steamfitter's union, the Church's social teaching continued to interest me keenly during the first three decades of my Jesuit life. But the civil rights and anti-Vietnam War movements found me pretty much of an onlooker, even though a number of our Jesuit scholastics at Woodstock had joined Dan and Phil Berrigan and their associates in demonstrations and civil disobedience.

So I was not a little surprised — and more than a little terrified — when Tom Quigley invited me to speak at the CICOP assembly, a forum for airing religious concerns about justice in the Americas. I asked myself what I was doing on the same platform with Gustavo Gutierrez, Rosemary Ruether, and other proponents of theologies of liberation. Very late I realized that my talk, on a theology of development, was on the program as a counterpiece to one by a Mexican Dominican on liberation. My presentation, subsequently published in the proceedings of the meeting, still appears to me attractive in its limpidity, but bland

116

and abstract, with no discernible passion for justice, and with little awareness of the sharp rejection of models of development by the budding liberation theology.[1] Even as proposed by Paul VI in 1967 in his Encyclical on the development of peoples, the development model was too reminiscent of the efforts of the Yankee colossus to meet Latin America's massive social problems with inept and degrading capitalistic solutions. Listening to Gutierrez must have rubbed off on me, for when I went to the Philippines the following year I devoted the principal talk to exploring the tensions between the theological models of development and liberation. I was intrigued by the possibility of taking some traditional dogmas, on the incarnation, redemption, and grace, together with the historical controversies surrounding them, and making them meaningful within a contemporary context.

Another contributing factor was my attraction to Augustine's redemption-centered theology of grace, which had first drawn me during my doctoral studies in Rome in 1952-1954 and which greatly influenced my teaching of the theology of grace at Woodstock from 1954 on. I had come to see Augustine as a brilliant interpreter of Paul and a champion of the paschal mystery, understood in terms of the "happy fault" celebrated each year in the Easter vigil. This influence tended to make me wary of models which were primarily developmental and which, in my view, tended to put the mystery of evil and human liberation from evil on the periphery of Christian consciousness. Thus, in 1967, I did a lengthy review of John Hick's book, *God and the Problem of Evil*, which, in playing Augustine off against Irenaeus, offered, in my view, a version of the gospel too bland for addressing the apocalyptic struggle of our times.[2]

This Augustinian cast of mind did not keep me from appreciating, from about 1955, Pierre Teilhard de Chardin's bold effort at a cosmic Christology. With a good many others I wondered whether this great scientist/mystic did justice in his synthesis to the immensity of evil in the world. Christopher Mooney's lucid study, *Teilhard de Chardin and the Mystery of*

Christ, had helped me appreciate that the French Jesuit was agonizingly conscious of the influence of evil in the world. Some years later, Karl Rahner's essay "Christology Within an Evolutionary Worldview" served to keep the development/liberation model prominent in my reflection. Moving towards the late seventies, I became better acquainted with the views of Johannes Metz, and had the privilege of conversing with him at a meeting of the National Sisters Vocation Conference in Cleveland in 1982. His critique of the bourgeois society included a critique of the idea of evolutionism prevalent in that society, and he called for a return to the apocalyptic perspectives of certain parts of the New Testament. This strengthened my attachment to the liberation model, as did my learning over the past several years from the tradition of non-violence as a Gospel mode of responding to evil. More recently, an embryonic acquaintance with the ecological views of Thomas Berry and Matthew Fox — to which I will allude in the final chapter — made me appreciate that the cosmological as well as the strictly anthropological aspects of the development/liberation tension needed attention. I will not here, however, be addressing the concerns raised by these more recent ecological models. In the following reflection I will be content to situate the development/liberation option within an older historical context, dealing in turn with the Incarnation/redemption tension debated by Scotists and Thomists from the late Middle Ages on, and with the theology of grace in its historical shift from the time of Augustine to the scholastic period. However remote these historical controversies might appear to be from our current social interests, they are relevant to the spiritual and pastoral implications of whatever developmental and/or liberational models we may prefer.

Recent Shifts in Theology

Quite a few theologies of development have been proposed in recent decades. It seems fair to say that the stimulus towards them has come first from the broad evolutionary world view resulting from the biological insights of Darwin and others, and later from the field of developmental psychology as it sought models for the growth of persons, more attuned to clinical experience. Beyond the specialized biological and psychological disciplines, however, evolution and development became major elements within our cultural consciousness and within the workings of the personal and collective unconscious. The special ethos of that portion of the Americas known as the United States of America provided a congenial milieu for the myth of evolution imported from the Continent. In Western society as a whole for most of the twentieth century, mindsets and lifestyles have been profoundly shaped by this myth; and, in social, political, and economic circles after World War II, the myth of development became the carrier of dreams of a better world, generating goal-setting, policies, and programs on a global scale. Those responsible for the Church's official social teaching soon grasped the aptness of this theme for articulating the Gospel message in today's language. Vatican II's *Constitution on the Church in the World of Today*, in somewhat Teilhardian fashion, spoke challengingly and optimistically (too optimistically, in the view of some Protestant commentators) of our responsibility to develop the creation according to the divine plan of salvation. While not taking sides in the quarrel between "Incarnationists" and "Eschatologists" which had existed in France and elsewhere since the forties, the Council tended to accent the continuity rather than the discontinuity which obtained between the course of history and the coming of the kingdom. Paul VI's Encyclical "On the Development of Peoples," in 1967, continued the favor shown in official Church circles to the model of development.

Such favor to the notion of development is rightly seen as situated within the broad current of accommodation of the post-feudal Church to the mentality of the Enlightenment. More than a century after Pius IX's *Syllabus of Errors* had condemned the proposition that the Roman pontiff could and should become reconciled with progress and liberalism, the official Church finally found its way to doing just that. But the ink was hardly dry on such openings to liberal Western society before this kind of language came in for criticism on the part of political and liberation theologians.

Johannes Metz has been particularly critical in linking evolutionary theologies of history with the bourgeois or middle class mentality which he sees as now needing to yield to a fresh appreciation of the role of the powerless in history.[3] He also judges that such theologies, especially as influenced by an existentialist preoccupation with the individual, become unfaithful to the deep eschatological and apocalyptic elements which make the Gospel such a radical message for our times.

Liberation theologies, on their side, have been wary of theologies of development partly because of the association of such theologies with the neo-colonialism by which the North, in the deceptively benign language of development, has continued to exploit the Third World for the benefit of the consumer society. A further point of criticism has been the inadequacy of the notion of development for describing the weight of structural evil present in today's oppression of the poor by the rich, and for calling forth the combative passions required if we are to deal effectively with the contradictions inherent in capitalistic society. Hence, in the view of Latin American theologians, the imperative is for a theology of liberation sharply contrasting with theologies of development. In the 1980s this development/liberation issue has perhaps passed its peak, but it is still possible to draw spiritual and pastoral profit from comparing and evaluating the two notions as models of personal and societal salvation.

Classical Theology: Incarnation Debate

One help towards such a comparison and evaluation consists in situating the endeavor within the context of the history of doctrine. In Christology and in the doctrine of grace, two contrasting positions, broadly corresponding to development and liberation, have contended for dominance. Sketching out these classic differences may throw some light on our current concerns.

Thomas Aquinas and his contemporaries posed the perennial question of the purpose of the Incarnation as, "If Adam ;had not sinner, would Christ have come?" Subsequent generations of scholastics, almost to our own day, expended enormous energy around this question. There is a sense in which it is an otiose question for, as Aquinas himself notes, we have no knowledge of God's choice in any order but our own, in which as a matter of fact Adam did sin and the Word was made flesh for our salvation. Such a reticence is consistent with what we saw in the last chapter, in Sertillanges' refusal to invade the divine planning room. Still, the question has considerable heuristic value, that is, playing with what might have been can deepen our grasp of what actually is. The classic Adam/Christ question compels the theologian to weigh and weight the different elements which constitute the present order of salvation, and also to risk speaking the language judged to be more congruous with the challenges of today.

The classic position identified as Scotistic (after Duns Scotus) or Franciscan, maintains that had Adam not sinned Christ would still have come. What is seen as primary in the actual order of salvation is the divinization of humankind and of the whole creation through the Incarnation. Such a language is certainly congruous with our popular image of Francis of Assisi, particularly of his "Canticle of the Sun" celebrating God's glory throughout the creation. Advocacy of the Scotistic view, especially when expressed along evolutionary or developmental lines, can neglect the place of the redemptive Cross in Francis' personal life, even to the point of neglecting his bearing the wounds of the Crucified one. Today Teilhard de Chardin is often presented as a twentieth century visionary and exponent of the Franciscan accent. He and others who make this option are especially fond of the passages in Ephesians and Colossians where the Pauline "cosmic Christology" appears.

The classic Thomist position, sometimes less diffident than Aquinas himself about dealing with the question, responds with him that apart from Adam's sin Christ would not have come, since our faith teaches that the purpose of the Incarnation is our redemption from sin.

Without elaborating a theological response to the question, I would say two things. First, when the insights of Sertillanges and Rahner presented in the previous chapter are taken as assumptions to any discussion of God's will and purpose, it becomes clear that the question is not about what God might have done in other circumstances, or about some sequence in the divine planning mind, anthropomorphically conceived; but rather it is about the relationships which obtain within the actual order of salvation. And second, the important question is which emphasis, on the development of creation or on liberation from evil, is spiritually and pastorally more suited to our present cultural context.

Within these two assumptions, I confess to a Thomistic — and, as I will later say — to an Augustinian bias. If only by way of accent, the Scotistic response seems to me to run too great a risk of relegating the struggle with and victory over evil to a secondary role in the process of salvation. While it does, with some plausibility, seek to incorporate the mystery of the cross and resurrection into its vision of a fulfilled universe, I find that primary energy in typical expressions of this view goes into the celebration of the evolutionary unfolding of the potential of the creation. Rather commonly, evil — whether of pain, death, or sin — appears as an almost inevitable flaw present in the early stages of an unfinished universe. And at times a polar conception of good and evil, light and darkness, drawn from non-Christian spiritualities or from Jungian psychology, is applied too smoothly to the stark mystery of iniquity described in the sources of Christian faith, and experienced in unprecedented massiveness in our own century.

The Thomistic view is not without its own risks; for example, of narrowing its gaze to the human aspects of the drama of redemptive Incarnation, neglecting the rich resources available in Scripture and tradition for a cosmic soteriology. Still, as I will say below, such risks (for which the Thomistic view is not without resources) are justified by the need to keep in view the demonic and tragic character of humankind's situation in our day. The traditional term "redemption" really stands for "liberation," and today, in my opinion, it is the language of liberation rather than the language of development which can generate the energies required by our global situation. Whatever readers may choose as their own language option, I hope that the classic Thomist-Scotist quarrel may be seen as shedding some light on our need to choose our language today.

Classical Theology: Grace, Healing or Elevating

A second historical theme can likewise assist this kind of discerning choice of theological models. Historians of the doctrine of grace have noted the contrast, first between Augustine and several of the Greek Fathers such as Gregory of Nyssa; and then, as the theology of grace developed in the West, between Augustine and what emerged in the High Middle Ages. A brief sketch of Augustine's model will help us begin to appreciate the relevancy of this development to the development/liberation option today.

Augustine's well known struggle with and victory over the flesh would lead us to expect his theology of grace to have the characteristics which in fact it has. It is in effect a celebration of "amazing grace," of the "happy fault," which the Church celebrates in the Easter vigil. For Augustine grace is less a principle of growth than a healing and liberating hand stretched out by God in Christ to rescue humankind from the mortal sickness and dark imprisonment which is our lot as a result of Adam's sin.

Augustine's entire theology of grace pivots about the radical discontinuity between the grace of the first and of the second Adam. The grace of paradise was, he wrote, *adiutorium sine quo non*, a necessary help towards sharing in divine life bestowed upon a human creature still innocent and therefore still capable of shaping life through the right use of free will. Far different is the *adiutorium quo*, the grace needed by a fallen race and gained through the victory of Christ over Satan. This is a grace which does not presuppose good will but bestows it. Echoing Paul's "it is God, for his own loving purpose, who puts both the will and the action into you" (Phillipians 2:13), Augustine is willing to take the risk of seeming to make God's gracious freedom substitute for the total absence of freedom in us sinners. Whatever the efficacy of his defense of his views of grace and predestination, first against Pelagians and then against otherwise friendly monks in Africa and southern France, Augustine sought to maintain a place for our free response to God's initiative; but he insisted that the freedom of the response to grace was itself unmerited grace.

This does not mean that the great bishop of Hippo did not maintain the possibility of our growing in the life of charity. But in all that he wrote, the accent falls on liberation from sin, not on development in grace; and he certainly had no room for any understanding of this time of pilgrimage which tended to reduce the place of conflict between sin and grace. Luther was not wrong, when he felt the call to accent human helplessness to seek or find God, in appealing not only to Paul but to Augustine.

While Augustine's theology of grace continued to influence the choice of models until and beyond the Council of Trent, scholastic thought in the Middle Ages moved towards more abstract models, and specifically towards the systematic distinction of natural and supernatural ends and orders. In the technical language of theology, "elevating" grace tended to overshadow "healing" grace. The radical insufficiency of any creature, angelic as well as human, for immediate participation in trinitarian life, became the primary basis for the necessity of grace; the need for grace based upon our radical sinfulness was pushed into the background. In such a shift, Roman Catholic theology, especially in the hands of the particular Jesuit tradition known as Molinism, virtually opted for development over liberation in conceptions of the life of grace. Compared with Paul and Augustine, as well as with the original impetus of the theology of the Reformers, this meant a more optimistic kind of language for describing the human condition. It is only in the present century, especially through theologies of liberation, that creational and developmental accents have had to yield a little to sin/grace models of the process of salvation.

Hence, in summary, both Christology and the theology of grace provide us with histories which foreshadow the present tension between models of development and liberation. The pivotal question in the choice of models seems to be the question of how seriously the reality of evil, and the force needed to overcome it, is taken. One notices, too, a generally greater focus on conflict in theologies of liberation than in theologies of development. Development theories take the risk of being bland, liberation theories the risk of being dour. Each view will seek to incorporate the central concerns of the opposite view.

Choosing Liberation Models for Today

From the viewpoint of spiritual and pastoral theology, what can we say about such an option between development and liberation in the sense here outlined? My first observation is that, as Augustine's personal history illustrates, our choices will be influenced by our personalities, our personal history, and cultural influences. But we also need to approach such theological choices with a discerning eye on the signs of our times. We are dealing not precisely with theological truth or error, correctness or incorrectness in our propositions, but rather with issues of truth as *praxis*, with fidelity to love as discerning choice. The question then becomes: what ways of structuring our speech about the mystery of salvation as it is being enacted in our society today promise to energize us spiritually and pastorally for the choices we need to make?

When the question is put in this way, my sympathies, doubtless influenced by personality, personal history, and cultural situation, draw me more to the language of liberation than to that of development. The model I choose should enable me to deal with the monstrous evils which have afflicted humankind in my lifetime: two World Wars, together with the Korean and Indochinese wars; Dachau and Hiroshima and Jonestown; the blood baths of Central America, Northern Ireland, and the Middle East; the threat of unspeakable evil hanging over all of us through the arms race and the militarism behind it; the devastation of the physical environment, all the more threatening for being almost unnoticed by the masses of people; the contempt in which our technological culture holds prisoners, the unborn, and those whom age or illness remove from the list of attractive producers and consumers; the increasing oppression of the poor by the rich on a global scale. When I am in the presence of such realities, viewed in their moral — not merely in their political or economic dimensions — I doubt that the energies needed to cope with them can be found in any predominantly developmental view. That is why, for all the enrichment it has brought, a Teilhardian perspective — despite Teilhard himself taking evil very seriously — can hardly, in my view, be our central recourse. Such efforts as those of John Hick and Matthew Fox, which I would situate essentially with developmental views, likewise seem to gloss over the enormity of the evil with which we grapple. If we are to meet the signs of our times, our primary models and metaphors will need to accent the eschatological and even the apocalyptic components of the Gospel. They will have to disengage more fully than they have from the blandness of evolutionism in its influence on Christian theology. And they will have to assimilate themes of discontinuity, impasse, dark night within a hope which is clearly differentiated from optimism.

Another aspect of the inadequacy of developmental models and of the need for liberational models is expressed by saying that the former characteristically fail to capitalize on the powerful energies contained in such human passions as fear, anger, and combativeness. These and similar gifts have been bestowed by God precisely for dealing with evil, either defensively, as in the case of fear, or offensively, as with anger and readiness to enter into combat. Developmental models which proceed from some kind of evolutionary hypothesis may theoretically acknowledge the need to struggle with the resistances built into the processes of history. But in its impact on those who are expected to act vigorously against such resistances, the language of development tends to invite optimism rather than hope. It draws upon the energies which derive from the expectation of a happy future, but not sufficiently on the energies generated in a desperate struggle with present or imminent evil. Hope begins where there are no grounds for optimism.

It is no accident that developmental theologies tend to emerge from academic or middle class milieus, whereas liberation theologies have their origin from groups that struggle with the experience of oppression — the economically and societally deprived of the Third World, blacks in our own country, women in society and in the Church. The history of such movements shows how risky are the language and strategies of liberation. From the standpoint of the Gospel, the greatest risk may be the temptation to resort to some species of violence, which in the long run capitulates to the cycle of oppression. Here is where I personally look to the struggle of women for liberation, to find radically different responses to this dilemma. In fact, I have to admit that the distinction of development and liberation as I have outlined it in this chapter most likely contains assumptions which stem from a masculine perspective which limits its power to enlighten. At any rate, this is as far as I have come.

Liberation for Spiritual and Pastoral Energy

How might the distinction of liberation and development affect spirituality and ministerial practice? In the former area its principal contribution may well be the raising of questions concerning our assumptions about spiritual growth. Let me examine the language of my spirituality to see which model is favored. Where the language is couched in exclusively developmental terms, where growth is conceived merely as the gradual transcending of immaturity or the flaws inevitably present in any evolutionary process leading to perfection, I need to ask whether I have not filtered out the power of the Cross of Christ. Evil, darkness, shadow, sin, enslavement, and consequently redemption, liberation, healing, forgiveness — these are terms which will have an important place in any spirituality which is attuned to the distress of our times.

Readiness for struggle and conflict, as well as a willingness to make a place for fear and anger, will also be signs of a spirituality of liberation. Both with respect to our own personhood and with respect to life in community and in society, we need to be wary of coming prematurely or in escapist fashion to postures of harmony and peace which repress our awareness of underlying conflict and doubt. Particularly where the spirituality of individuals and groups interacts with the surrounding society and culture, the peace which is Christ's gift to his friends will be precarious and embattled. Spirituality today seems called to be countercultural and even, in a quite different fashion from in the past, unworldly. This last term may appear abhorrent to those set free, in the period of "Christian secularity," from an alienation from modernity that stemmed more from medieval sacralism than from the demands of the Gospel. But it is not without reason that the New Testament sometimes speaks of the world pejoratively. Paul warns against the "present age," a term which designates the unredeemed dimensions of the creation that seek to quench the new life of the "future age" already present.

Something similar needs to be said with respect to ministerial accents. Surely our middle class Christian people need the consolation of the Gospel. But, unlike the poor, it is easy for them to find other securities than what Jesus offers to those who follow him. Unless they are taught to see the snares of cultural illusion and addiction in our society today, eventually the impact of the Gospel on their lives will be reduced to mere ritual and superficial observance. Through every vehicle of ministry they need to deal with these hazards, namely finding that "option for the poor" which will enable them to share in the Good News.

How can the Cross of Jesus Christ, its power to liberate from every form of death and evil, and the absolute necessity for experiencing the distinctive peace which the risen Lord bestows, be mediated through all the vehicles of Christian ministry today? Within a liberation model chosen as basis for pastoral ministry, this is the question which calls for ongoing response from the ministers of the Church.

Questions for Reflection

For personal spirituality:

1. When I examine my favorite images and metaphors for the

spiritual journey, do they suggest that either development or liberation is predominant in my spirituality?
2. What emerges when I ask a similar question about my favorite scriptural passages?
3. When I experience injustice or any kind of human conflict, am I able effectively to draw upon the resources of my human fear and anger for a courageous response?

For ministry:

1. Examine your preaching and teaching and see whether developmental or liberational concepts and images prevail, and ask whether such favor meets your analysis of the needs of those to whom you speak.
2. In recommending social action against injustice, does the possibility of civil disobedience or other forms of non-violent protest have a place?
3. In your appraisal of the present condition of American public life and culture, do you look for reform or revolution, for continuity or discontinuity with present attitudes and structures?

9
Love/Justice

The four years I spent at the Woodstock Theological Center in Washington from 1977 to 1981 were more fruitful in teaching me something about myself than was any theological production. Especially through participating in the Center's most ambitious project, on human rights in the Americas (which eventually yielded two volumes of essays by about twenty collaborators), I came fully to realize that research and scholarship were not really what I cared to do or could do well. Quite apart from sloppy habits of reading and writing built up over a period of decades, I found myself less interested in advancing human knowledge in some specific discipline than in exploring and sharing insights for whose validation and acceptance by an academic peer group I cared little. My efforts to make a respectable contribution to our interdisciplinary human rights project were painful, halting, and diffident.

The mouse that finally emerged from my mountainous groanings was a sprawling essay for which I have still a good deal of personal affection but which seems to have left the academic and political world unmoved.[1] Its thesis was that every human being has a basic human need, and therefore a basic human right, not merely to receive adequate nutrition but to share meals in dignity with one's family or other human community. The experience of sharing food and drink had engaged my interest for several years. In 1976, at Gonzaga Center in Monroe, New York, Peter Henriot, Sister Marita Carew, and I had conducted a rich weekend program which sought to integrate a Eucharistic perspective with concern for world hunger. Later, at an Ignatian symposium at Regis College in Toronto in 1981, I would present a paper on the "Rules With Regard to Eating" of Ignatius' *Spiritual Exercises*, attempting to show how a her-

130

meneutical revival of these all but unnoticed directives could contribute to the quest for justice today.[2]

The Woodstock human rights project saw me, over a period of a few years, go off on several tangents and false starts. One of these explorations dealt with the relationship of love and justice. This particular adventure originated in an unsolicited question which appeared in my imagination one day, "Is there a basic human right to love?" The question excited me partly because it challenged what I perceived as a too facile assumption that love and justice are alternatives. More specifically, the theme of love as a political virtue, not merely a private one, drew me to extensive reading and reflection. What I found in Paul Tillich and Robert Johann persuaded me that I was on a good track.[3] My human rights essay made only passing use of these love/justice reflections. But subsequently I embodied a part of these reflections in an essay for *The Way*, a British spiritual journal.[4] I have saved those love/justice notes and have retained some hope of doing a little book for the general public, calling for the admission of love as communion into our political life. What follows may give an idea of what, in more amplified form, such a book might contain.

Love: Desire for Communion

Let me begin with love. Though it is not strictly definable, love still needs to be analyzed in its relationship to justice. For the theological reflection pursued in these pages, the common human experience of love, especially within the context of Christian commitment, serves as an appropriate starting point, while allowing our revelatory personal experience to be monitored by recourse to Scripture and tradition. I offer the following reflection so that readers may evaluate it as descriptive or not of what they experience when they are open to love from God and other people, and when they struggle to return love for love.

Love does indeed make the world go round. It is a power, an energy, which more than any other shapes our life for better or for worse. It might even be claimed that no other energy flows except in relation to the flow of love. *Amor meus pondus meum*, wrote Augustine (literally, my love is my gravity, my burden). The gravity of life, the basic law of attraction, is the pull of love. Another classic phrase of Augustine, as he pondered John 6:44 ("No one can come to me unless the Father who has sent me draw him"), was: *Trahit sua quemque voluntas* ("It is will that draws each of us"). As rhetorician he played with *voluntas* (will) and *voluptas* (pleasure, desire) in order to emphasize the role of appetite and attraction in the dynamism of love. Augustine's combination of the cosmic model of gravity and the psychological model of desire brings us back to the motif of power/energy, the integrating theme in these essays. Love is the most powerful energizing force in creation, reflective of the God who *is* love.

Since Anders Nygren's classic *Agape and Eros*, Augustine has often been depicted as something of a villain in his conception of love as appetite or desire. He is sometimes accused of reducing Christian *agape*, God's utterly altrustic and undeserved love poured forth in our hearts through the Holy Spirit (Galatians 4:6), to the self-interested *eros* of the Greek philosophers — natural and even tainted with sin, of which alone we are capable without God's transforming grace.

At the risk of too sweeping a generalization, I think we can say that, with significant differences, Nygren's sharp contrast of *agape* and *eros* has prevailed in the mainstream of Protestant theology and has recently had considerable influence in Roman Catholic circles. To the extent to which this is true, the chosen risks of this prevalent view have tended to dichotomize self-interest and altruism in interpersonal love, and directly or indirectly to separate the private and personal from the public and political spheres of human existence. Accordingly, in a rather common version of this line of thought, love — or at least altruistic love — stops at the threshold of political life, which is conceived as the home court of a tough justice that is far removed from *agape*.

In contrast, I prefer to work from a notion of love which has roots both in common human experience and in the Bible, and which I believe also squares with a healthy psychology of development. This viewpoint would see the altruism/self-interest distinction as secondary to something more powerful, namely the drive for *communion* which is the heart of love both human and divine.

Human love represents, within the creation, the peak instance of a drive towards communion that is inscribed on every atom and molecule in the universe. To adapt another of Augustine's famous dictums, God has made us for communion, and our hearts are restless until they are fulfilled in communion — agreement of mind, solidarity of will, harmony of heart, with one another and with God. Among Catholic theologians of the present century, Emile Mersch, Pierre Teilhard de Chardin, and Hans Urs von Balthasar, together with the philosopher Gabriel Marcel, stand out in the strength of their insistence that Christian existence is coexistence, that to be is to be with and in one another.

So far as the relationship of self-directed and other-directed love is concerned, it is an important but relative distinction, and a distinction not between alternative acts of love so much as between different dimensions of each act of love. Legitimate self-interest is an inescapable part of all creaturely love. The absolute altruism of God is beyond the reach of every finite creature. Though it does not find explicit expression in the ten commandments or in Jesus' new commandment of love, self-love — responsibility for one's own well-being — is built into the covenant of creation. Even the supreme instance of selfless love, laying down one's life for the neighbor, is an instance of radical self-interest. So far as I know, Jesus never admonished anyone for aspiring to personal greatness or fulfillment, though he did make it clear where these were to be found, and at what price. Psychologically, growth in holiness does bring a certain relinquishment of preoccupation with one's own less radical needs. But generous sacrifice for others is empowered, not enervated, by the passionate desire to find one's own life and to exercise it to the full. I believe that modern psychology, when it berates narcissim, sees in it not an excessive self-love but rather a masked effort to escape the pain resulting from a diminished sense of self-worth.

The coexistence of altruism and self-interest at the heart of the drive for communion can be further appreciated if this dynamic movement of the human spirit is approached from the standpoint of *gift*. When Ignatius of Loyola, in his "Contemplation for Gaining Divine Love," describes the love which is being sought as a consummate grace, he does so in the language of mutual self-giving: ". . . love consists in a mutual sharing of goods, for example, the lover gives and shares with the beloved what he possesses, or something of that which he has or is able to give; and vice versa, the beloved shares with the lover . . . Thus, one always gives to the other" (*Spiritual Exercises* n. 231).

An even more celebrated prayer of Francis of Assisi signalizes the paradoxical character of this mutual gift relationship: it is in giving to others that we receive. The *agape* described by Paul as the better gift is indeed altruistic in nature, in that it truly puts the radical good of the other ahead of our own less radical good. But it is also, paradoxically, the supreme instance of a healthy and holy desire for life and fullness for oneself.

In all its key elements — the drive towards communion, the desire and willingness to be in a mutual gift relationship, and the commingling of both altruistic and self-regarding motivations — this notion of love stands up well to the test of common human experience, as well as to the exigency of the *agape* which consciously proceeds from Christian faith. In the simple offering of an alms, in non-violent postures toward those who would be our enemies, in the intimacy of deepest friendship and marital love, we do experience, in a variety of emotional moods, the gift of communion in a love that is both desire for our own good and benevolence towards the other. As Paul Tillich has said, the three classic aspects of love, *amor concupiscentiae* (love of self-interested desire), *amor amicitiae* (love of friendship), and *amor benevolentiae* (love of benevolence) are only that, aspects of love, not three disjunctive kinds of human behavior.

The Walden Model of Love

This understanding of love as communion can be further elaborated with the help of a few of the basic models described in previous chapters, particularly the Walden model and the tetrad suggested by the Jungian functions. A word about each of these will prepare for our comparison of love with justice.

The Walden model, it will be recalled, spoke of the interaction of solitude, friendship, and society; or of intrapersonal, interpersonal, and societal dimensions of behavior. Love as communion is most easily understood as the heart of friendship, the center of our interpersonal existence. But it is also verified in an extended sense in our attitudes and behavior towards ourselves, and is susceptible to embodiment in societal structures and institutions.

Love as intrapersonal communion has to do with loving oneself. It has often been noted that, in the second great commandment given in the dialogue between Jesus and the scribe, love for oneself is presupposed rather than formally commanded. Yet loving oneself is in fact a grave commandment of God who gives each of us stewardship over God's image within us. We are responsible and accountable for developing that personal image towards greater likeness to God. In order that God might give us himself in a supreme and total communion, he needed first to give us ourselves as subjects capable of receiving and responding to his self-gift. That this drive towards communion with ourselves is inherent in our nature is confirmed by what psychology tells us about the terrible contagion of evil that is set loose when people do not love themselves. The linkage, both spiritual and psychological, between communion with oneself and with the neighbor, and between alienation from oneself and from the neighbor, is too well known to need further elaboration. In a way, we are back to our previous discussion of the coexistence of the self-regarding and altruistic aspects always to be found in genuine human love.

What does call for further explanation is the fact that love as communion can, and in fact does, take on a societal or political

character. Even among many who readily agree that structures
and institutions can be just or unjust, there is a certain reluctance to admit the same for love. But, given the validity of the
basic model of the human which I have described in Chapter 3,
there is no reason to deny to love the triadic character of all that
is human.

Moreover, our experience confirms that we do in fact create
climates of life precisely in order to facilitate the communion
with one another to which we feel called. Examples run all the
way from table etiquette and conventional forms of meeting and
greeting others to providing kneeling buses and ramps for the
elderly and disabled. That love is embodied in such structures
through the mediation of other less transcendent virtues such
as courtesy, compassion, and justice, does not deny that such
structures are mediations of and concrete participations in the
communion of hearts which both precedes and follows their creation. The good news here is that structures and institutions can
be a kind of sacrament, effective signs of the love which creates
them and which is itself enhanced by them.

It follows, I believe, that *political love* is a valid and helpful
concept. Especially in a highly individualistic, competitive, and
presently narcissistic society, this term reminds us that claims
upon others in the form of individual rights presuppose a basic
bondedness with these others. If my relationship with you does
not contain, at its core, a command that we acknowledge and
foster a basic communion which we have as members of humankind, why should your need constitute a claim on my disposing
of my human energies?

The love that makes the world go round is, then, a love that is
simultaneously intrapersonal, interpersonal, and societal or
political. The quality of the actual communion present in each of
these three dimensions will condition the quality of the communion present in the other two. Love of self and of the neighbor, and the embodiment of both in the structures of political
love, constitute the integral communion to which we are called.

Functions in Love

The four Jungian functions, which provided the model for Chapter 3, can now be brought to bear on this understanding of love as communion. In fact, in speaking of the correlation of justice with the thinking function, that chapter has anticipated what I will say shortly about the relationship of love and justice. But now I would like to draw more fully on the insight of Harold Grant in his correlation of the four Jungian functions with the four modalities of love contained in the first great commandment of love (Mark 12:30; Luke 10:27; see Deuteronomy 6:5). Loving with one's whole *heart* is correlated with the *feeling* function, which has directly to do with intimacy. Loving with one's whole *soul* (or spirit) correlates with the dreaming hope characteristic of the *intuiting* function; it is with the soul or spirit that we aspire to future good for ourselves or others. Loving with one's whole *strength* correlates with the *thinking* function, with its resources of power and toughness. And loving with one's whole *mind* correlates with the *sensing* function, through which we exercise a practical, down-to-earth attention to the one whom we love.

The special value of this holistic approach to love is that it provides a healthy challenge to our tendency to reduce love to tenderness and sentiment. Our actual experience of love discloses that it sometimes needs to be tough as well as tender. The Bible tells us that the Lord chastises or disciplines those whom he loves (Hebrews 12:6; see Proverbs 3:12). Also, by insisting that the exercise of the two perceiving functions, sensing and intuiting, are intrinsic to the communion of love, the model provides for the mutual receptivity, the contemplative gaze, without which love cannot be integral. If love is mutual self-giving, it needs also to be mutual readiness to receive. It may be, as Paul recalls from an apocryphal saying of Jesus, that it is better to give than to receive; but for some personalities it is more difficult to receive than to give. Often, in fact, the best gift we can bestow on others consists simply in listening, gazing, letting them be themselves, and letting them give generously to us. I will never forget reading in a marriage manual over three decades ago the story of a husband who eventually drove his wife to divorce him because he insisted on caring for her needs to the full while not permitting her to do anything for him.

By combining this model with the Walden model, love as communion appears even more in its rich complexity. While its central verification is in interpersonal love, the four faces of love are also involved in our love for ourselves as well as in the political dimension of love. This last aspect calls for some amplification. I am saying that the embodiment of communion in various societal climates will contain all four facets of love — heart, mind, strength, and soul. For example, social welfare programs need not merely to provide benefits for the poor but to be concretely expressive of a dynamic hope that the poor are given the necessary conditions provided with the help of public assistance, of directing their own lives in a healthy way. The dark side of the welfare state has been its subtle disregard for the powerful energies for life present in the poor. At its worst, through an institutionalism of "do-good-ism" that neglects the riches possessed by the poor, it has communicated to them a denigrating image of themselves and invited them to continue in a demeaning dependency on others. In contrast, a program like the U.S. Catholic Bishops' *Campaign for Human Development* bases its exercise of societal love on the premise that the poor, once enabled, have the power to shape their own lives. The political love which embodies a dreeaming hope will call forth, not replace, the dreaming hoe which still burns humanly beneath the ashes of the grossest poverty.

Similarly, societal communion structures will not be soft and sentimental in the name of compassion, but will encourage a certain toughness and readiness for struggle — qualities associated with the thinking function. The principle of fairness in our society is a major instance of how attitudes of communion need to find societal expressions which balance intimacy with respect and human dignity.

Justice Comes From Love

This last consideration brings us to a point where we can speak more directly of the relationship of love and justice. Especially within the fourfold approach to love through correlation with the Jungian functions, it is at once apparent that love and justice cannot be totally extrinsic to each other. From Paul Tillich and Robert Johann, and to some extent from Jacques Maritain, I have gained enlightenment and confirmation for this conviction. When love is viewed comprehensively, it is seen to contain justice as a constitutive dimension. More particularly, the active or responsive dimension of love contains two qualities which exist in a complementarity and tension with each other. Love is indeed defined as a dynamic movement towards ever fuller communion with the beloved. But where there is a question of subjects endowed with consciousness and freedom, this communion takes place not by absorption but by a paradoxical movement towards affirming the other as other. This firm will that the beloved other be other, not absorbed into the being of the lover, is the virtue of justice, which wills to each person what is due, what is required for that person to be a unique self. Justice thus becomes an exigency of true love, and communion requires distinction.

Teilhard brilliantly formulated this aspect of cosmic love: *Unity differentiates.* Karl Rahner's paradigm of creation/Incarnation, seen in Chapter 7, according to which radical dependency on God and radical autonomy coexist in the creature in direct — and not in inverse — proportion, has its counterpart here with respect also to communion among creatures. The will to be one with another carries with it a will to acknowledge that, even in the most intimate communion of love, the other remains a unique subject.

As there is no justice without love, so there is no love without justice. In this basic sense I would not agree with the proposition that love goes beyond justice, even though the altruistic element in every love/justice relationship is signaled more by the term love than by the term justice. As I tried to develop in my article in *The Way*, the peace which names total communion can come only through the simultaneous working of tender love and firm justice. When this dynamic interplay of love and justice is integrated with the interplay of solitude, friendship, and society, we have, I believe, a rather comprehensive model which can guide both spiritual development and ministerial practice. Here are a few suggestions under each heading.

Spiritual Balance

First, those who are seeking to grow in the Spirit might well ask for the grace of self-knowledge in the matter of love and justice, particularly in view of their personality types. Experience seems to show that among those drawn to prayer and spiritual development, a decided majority sees God and Jesus far more as tender and compassionate than as righteous and "tough." The ideal of virtue which impels them seems also to accent intimacy and harmony with others over respect for and vigorous defense of rights. It may be fair to say that justice, unlike love, appears to such people not as a spiritual category but as a moral one. It is considered to be a presupposition, not a constitutive element, of the spiritual quest, which is conceived to go beyond justice in generous, "superogatory" love. If what has been said here of love and justice is correct, such attitudes deprive those who entertain them of a balance and tension which might enrich their journey of faith. And at a certain point in their lives, perhaps in the middle years, when the passion for justice begins spontaneously to emerge in their consciousness, a failure to appreciate that justice is a constitutive dimension of love might block their realization that a singular grace of development is being offered to them.

A second practical value of the love/justice model for spiritual growth is that it can alert members of a family or other community to a frequent deficiency in community life, namely the neglect of order, discipline, appropriate structures and rituals, and the like. Especially when romantic or sentimental feelings have been strong in the initiatives which gave birth to a particular group, partial or total shipwreck often awaits the well-intentioned and good-hearted membership of the community because their anticipations have lacked balance. "All you really need is love" is an acceptable axiom, but only on the proviso that love be understood as comprehensive of justice, fairness, and provision for sound societal structures. Sometimes the success of a community or of a ministerial team will be contingent on the group having — and listening to — a member with a developed sense of justice, order, and truth. In the absence of such a member, the community will need consciously to cultivate such qualities in itself. In either case, it is important that community life not be narrowed by a stereotype of communion which makes no room for the assertive handling of conflict.

Justice for Ministry

One important area of ministerial practice which can be helped by reflection on the love/justice relationship is the ministry of counselling married or to-be-married partners. The model which sees justice as an intrinsic dimension of love calls those who share sexual intimacy to respect each other, no less than to be tender towards each other. While marriage is a total sharing of life, it does not fare well when this is understood as being incompatible with a certain distance and autonomy allowed to each partner. Respect for uniqueness will find many practical expressions, depending on social and economic circumstances. Husband and wife need not always find their leisure and recreation in the same ways. Political differences and even some healthy arguments over politics are legitimate. And it is important that issues of fairness and respect not be swept under the rug but made part of ordinary communication.

Pastors who are dealing with troubled partners in marriage or with candidates for marriage will do well also to attend to the personality types of the partners. When the rule of "opposites attract" seems to be the case, it can be advisable to help the couple appreciate that the source of any tensions they experience may be not malice but rather personality differences. If, for example, a feeling spouse, whether husband or wife, learns from the thinking partner how to be more truthful and just, and the other in turn learns how to be more expressive of feelings of intimacy, many a marriage can be stabilized and enriched. Something similar may be said about parents providing a balanced emotional and social climate for their children, especially if the children differ notably from the parents in their personalities.

Finally, the basic and long term goals and objectives of any ministerial unit — parish, diocese, or national Church — will best be formulated by including the language of justice, love, and peace. This is in fact what has taken place in the Roman Catholic Church in the past century. The second synod of bishops in 1971 articulated this in language that has become almost a credo of social commitment: "Action on behalf of justice and participation in the transformation of the world fully appear to us as a constitutive dimension of the preaching of the Gospel, or, in other words, of the Church's mission for the redemption of the human race and its liberation from every oppressive situation." What the Spirit has brought to a fuller consciousness is that justice in the world and in the Church is not a mere facilitating condition for the living of the Kingdom here and now, but rather an intrinsic component of that life. Truly, justice and peace have embraced (Psalm 85:10).

Questions for Reflection

For personal spirituality:

1. How well do I practice love/justice towards myself? For example, do I treat my body and its well-being fairly.?
2. In relating to others, especially those with whom I am most intimate, does my desire for communion carry with it a respect for their autonomy?
3. Is concern for justice in society and in the Church an element in my personal spirituality? How is it exercised?

For ministry:

1. In our preaching, religious education, or counselling, is the call to love inclusive of the call to work for justice?
2. Are the structures and institutions with which I am associated fully respectful of people's rights?

10
The Pastoral Circle

In late summer of 1978, I was one of numerous guests at a joint assembly in Cleveland of the *Leadership Conference of Women Religious* and the *Conference of Major Superiors of Men*. The theme of the program was "Convergence and Solidarity." It was possibly the most skillfully designed and carefully prepared meeting I have ever experienced. With the help of the staff of the Center of Concern, the planners had created a process in four stages which went back and forth from the platform — on which speakers from diverse international cultures set the tone — to a hundred tables of ten persons each on the huge floor of the Cleveland convention center. This was my first introduction to a model of pastoral discernment named at one time "the praxis cycle" but now well known as "the pastoral circle." Subsequently developed by the Center of Concern, and especially by Joe Holland and Peter Henriot, this model figured prominently in several enterprises in which I have been involved.

At the Woodstock Theological Center later in 1978, I helped to launch a project on theological reflection which made a great deal of the pastoral circle. Two years of intense dialogue among a dozen people, including Joe Holland, bore fruit in a volume, *Tracing the Spirit*, edited by Jim Hug and published in 1983 by Paulist. During the same period, a group of six Jesuits, including Peter Henriot and myself, put together for our U.S. provincials a set of essays entitled, *The Context of Our Ministries*, which was published by the Jesuit Conference in 1981. It too was structured around the pastoral circle. More recently, after moving back to New York City in 1982, I met for several months with the staff of the Intercommunity Center for Justice and Peace, an institution sponsored by religious communities in the metropolitan New York area. The staff was already familiar with the model, and was seeking to develop closer ties between social analysis and theological reflection. Since then I have found myself using this process often in talks and workshops, notably in a rich week's experience with Ursulines at Walden, New York in 1982, a workshop with Margaret Galiardi at St. Joseph's University in Philadelphia in 1985, and two workshops with the bishops and major superiors of women of Michigan in 1985 and 1986.

Although this chapter will be detailing a method created by others, I have for almost a decade tried to integrate the model with two or three others, elsewhere described in this book. My essay in *Tracing the Spirit*, entitled "A New Way in Theology," has anticipated much of what I will now be saying. But the most personal aspect of my attachment to this model stems from my participation in 1974-75 in the 32nd General Congregation of the Society of Jesus. The principal document of that gathering, "Our Mission Today: the Service of Faith and the Promotion of Justice," in its key statement, called for a method of "deepening awareness" and "apostolic discernment." Subsequently our then Jesuit General, Pedro Arrupe, called attention to the centrality of that section of the document, and asserted (with allusion to Marshall McLuhan's famous dictum) "the method is the message."

I have come to believe strongly that the seriousness of any faith/justice endeavor will be proportionate to the care and perseverance shown in sustaining an appropriate method. Part of this conviction stems from attending to the careful attention to method shown by St. Ignatius in the *Spiritual Exercises*. The power of those exercises stems largely from this concern for method. Similarly, I believe that our energies for social transformation can be sustained only with the help of such a method as the pastoral circle. My present anxieties about the depth and tenacity of the commitment to justice of us Jesuits stems largely from what appears to be our deep reluctance to be faithful to an integral method of contemporary social discernment. But I continue to live in hope. Perhaps it is only when we see the fruits of efforts made by others to develop and apply the tools which we have helped to design that we will be convinced of their value and necessity.

A New Way of Theologizing

History reminds us that theology is not monolithic. As a vehicle of evangelization both within and without, its quest for the appropriate wording of the mystery of faith has taken place in diverse social and cultural contexts, in pursuit of many specific types of understanding, and employing a rich variety of appropriate methods. The locus, literal and metaphorical, of any theological endeavor will shape its role and purpose at any given stage of history. At various periods the residences of bishops (think of Augustine at Hippo), the monastery (Anselm), the medieval university (Aquinas and Bonaventure), the post-Tridentine seminary (Karl Rahner and Bernard Lonergan), the divinity school at a secular university (Paul Tillich) have been the sites of widely differing approaches to faith's search for understanding. There is really no such thing as *the* method of theology in any concrete sense. Methods, models, paradigms, emerge in the flow of history. They need always to be subjected to careful scrutiny. But we ought to beware of judging any way in theology by criteria proper to some other way.

I believe that recent decades in Church history have witnessed the emergence of a new way in theology, for which the term theological reflection seems appropriate. As I described this new way in my essay in *Tracing the Spirit*:

> The distinctiveness of this new way can be described from several standpoints. First, its *locus* or situation is not the seminary, the university campus, the Roman curia, but some kind of basic community. Second, its primary *agent* is not the professionally trained theologian, research scholar, or someone juridically entrusted with a canonical mission to theologize in immediate service to the hierarchical Church. Rather it is the basic community, its mem-

bers theologizing together in virtue of the baptismal and confirmational imperative to render an account to themselves and others of their faith. Third, its *goal* is pastoral action or praxis of the community in the Church as it touches the world. Fourth, its *method*, appropriate to the locus, agent, and goal, may be broadly described as a *common Christian reflection on revelatory experience* (including especially the "signs of the times") *interpreted with the help of social analysis and on the basis of Scripture and tradition, with a view to Christian action in the world.*[1]

In the pastoral circle, this new way in theology has found a promising concrete method which deserves to be understood, tested, and elaborated on the basis of further experience. The method is constituted as a recurring interaction between four kinds of theological behavior, designated respectively as: 1) experience (or "insertion"); 2) social analysis; 3) theological reflection; 4) pastoral decision. I refer interested readers to further elaborations of the model in the readings already referred to. Here I will describe the process generally while attending to the linkages with some of the other models treated in this volume.

Here are two preliminary observations:

First, the *entire* pastoral circle, not merely the phase designated as theological reflection, is a theological exercise of faith. It is important, for example, that we not identify the social analysis phase with the mere utilization of the social sciences in order to apply Christian principles to the social order. The analysis characteristic of the pastoral circle is Christian analysis, and is consciously and strongly influenced by the same faith commitment which guides the other phases of the process. I will return to this distinction of Christian analysis from the use of the social sciences later. The point now is that the entire process is theological, that is, an exercise of faith in search of understanding.

Second, while it is convenient to single out four aspects of the circle and to assign them a certain sequence, every concrete embodiment of the method will be more complex and more flexible than might at first appear. For example, as a group approaches commitment to a specific choice, it may wish to energize or detach itself by going back, with the help of Scripture, to some form of sharing individual stories or the common story. Especially because principles and methods of the discernment of spirits are involved, a sound method requires that the group remain continually sensitive to movements of the Holy Spirit throughout the decisional process.

Description of Theological Reflection

With these two preliminary remarks, let me proceed to each of the four phases or aspects of the pastoral circle.

1. Experience.

It is a major feature of theological reflection as a new way of theology that it presupposes God's ongoing revelation as mediated through every facet of human experience. This major current in modern theology taps into a broader prizing of individual and group experience in modern culture, and helps to distinguish theological reflection from both dogmatic and academic theologies, neither of which made common revelatory experience a theological source. With respect to academic theology, this becomes clear when we distinguish the *experiential* and the *empirical* aspects of human experience. Academic theology, in turning from a purely deductive method, has certainly prized the empirical approach which it has learned from secular disciplines. But it rarely draws upon the experiential channels of revelation.

> The empirical is primarily concerned with data, the factual, the accurate description of inner and outer phenomena. It allies sense (and instrumental extensions of the senses) and reason in an effort to understand and shape reality with as much detach-

ment from personal feeling and group bias as possible. The experiential referent, in contrast, draws on
sense and other experiences with a frank acceptance
of "reasons of the heart." It revels in what is unique,
personal, subjective. Not clinical experiment but
story-telling and artistic creation are its chosen vehicles.[2]

Most helpful in this theological mining of experience are different ways of keeping the past present, e.g., photo albums and dis-
plays, tape recordings, traditional songs, celebrations of annual
feasts, the keeping of archives, and not least by any means, the
presence of "old timers" who are walking embodiments of the
heritage.

Those who identify theology exclusively with an academic
model may be skeptical of calling such behavior theological or
even theologal. But in the total enterprise of grass-roots theological reflection engaged in by a Christian community, there is
probably no single element more important than the retrieval of
the meaningful past and its reshaping to meet present exigencies for the sake of a better future. In Jungian terms, here is
where the feeling function makes a distinctive contribution. The
values which have shaped the community and its members are
made available through story; thereby bonds of solidarity are
made stronger, firmer. Ample time needs to be given to both individual stories and the common story. I have found it helpful,
for example, after individuals (especially introverts) have had a
chance to recall the past in solitude, to let people in small groups
share with one another their personal history touching a theme
like violence and non-violence, or the place of meals in the life of
a family. Parish communities will be similarly energized when
appropriate ways are found to celebrate the history of the
parish. At St. Francis Xavier parish, in downtown Manhattan,
the Xavier Dance Company several years ago helped parishioners celebrate the hundredth anniversary of the church.

It is important that sad as well as happy memories be celebrated. Especially where resentment, anger, and fear have been

buried within individuals or the community as a whole, powerful underground blocks to decision will darken and frustrate the common endeavor. Through the charismatic movement we have come to appreciate the crucial importance of the healing of memories in the formation of apostolic communities. Sometimes drawing upon the reconciliation rites of the Church, such celebrations of healing and forgiveness can be powerful sources of new energy. It is not that fear and anger will cease to figure in people's lives. It would be unfortunate if this were the case, because these negative emotions are precious gifts of God bestowed on us for dealing with evil. The grace to be sought is rather the transformation of fear and anger from being dangerous instruments of violence to being elements of the courage and hope which every community needs for its struggle with the principalities and powers.

2. Social analysis

When a group moves from sharing experience to engaging in social analysis, a decided shift of mood and climate takes place, from the subjective to the objective, from feeling to thinking, from story to analysis, from the experiential to the empirical, from affective attachment to rational detachment. This is not to say that social analysis is detached in the sense of being "value-free," that is, uninfluenced by the value biases of the participants. But now people are being asked to detach themselves from the highly personal aspects of their own stories, and to look out at their world, at the various contexts of their personal lives. For example, from telling and hearing stories about their personal experience of violence, they now need to analyze how violence occurs in the city, the nation, the world. What are some of the generalizations they can make regarding the incidence of violence, the causes of violence, and the connection between violence and other social evils? Is violence itself a concept which calls for nuance and differentiation? What is the historical line of the escalation of violence in the last decade, or in the present century? For example, have the several large-scale wars of our era, in addition to the violence contained within them, spawned psychological and social violence within the consciousness and the unconscious of the returning veterans?

From a Jungian standpoint, social analysis enlists the contribution of the sensing and thinking functions. Here the empirical, rather than the experiential, side of experience is relevant. Both within the daily lives of participants and in the results of scholarly research which they may choose to employ, factual data and careful descriptions of phenomena are enlisted in the process. Such material is then taken up into rational analysis, the work of objectivization, generalization, contextualization, and the establishment of causal linkages among the many complex elements of the situation being studied. Such theological behavior calls for a mood that is rational, cool, emotionally detached. This means that serious social analysis is, for a majority of Church people, a difficult if rewarding discipline. Most of us are given, by personality and religious commitment, to making ready value judgments, and are prone to moralize at the drop of a hat. Our tender compassion, as well as the passion for justice which we bring to the total process, are valuable gifts. But there is a time for everything, and without being too wooden or rigid we can say that the social analysis phase of the pastoral circle is primarily an exercise of the thinking function, supported especially by the sensing function.

This is not to say, let me repeat, that social analysis proceeds independently of the values we hold dear, or that it is not a theological exercise of faith. Our commitment to the Gospel, and the effect in us of our own personal salvation history — both of which involved the feeling function — will significantly affect the way we practice social analysis. So will our faith considered as a vision of what life is meant to be — here the intuiting function is engaged — as well as faith's daily attentiveness to the practicalities of life — requiring use of the sensing function. The questions we raise in social analysis; the language we choose for formulating those questions; the facets of political, economic, social, cultural life to which we think it worth while to attend; all are crucial elements in any social analysis. The world's history is shaped not only by the answers we give to our public problems but by the choice of problems to answer. Our value commitment, our ideology, will generally direct our gaze towards this rather than that problem, and will often suggest a distinctive way of linking one problem with another. For example, a group whose experience and value commitment are predominantly feminist will have a basic perspective or horizon different from a group coming together on the basis of racial or class injustice. Thus social analysis, like each of the other phases of the pastoral circle, does not stand by itself in isolation. Still, it needs to be faithful to its predominantly empirical and rational character if it is to make its distinctive contribution to the total process.

It will be clear from several of the reading references of this chapter that social analysis contains several differentiated fields of exercise; for example, political, economic, psychosocial, cultural, religious. Within each of these fields there may be even more specific areas to be examined. For example, an analysis of violence might find itself helped by demography as it indicates a linkage between population shifts and growth in violence. Cultural analysis is an area which needs special attention, and it may well provide the base for integrating the total exercise of analysis. The centrality of culture will appear more fully in the final chapter.

One more remark on this second phase of the pastoral circle: It is here that most groups may be tempted to an unwarranted diffidence regarding their own competence, and to an excessive or rather misplaced recourse to experts whose professional analysis is permitted to substitute for the admittedly amateur analysis of the group. This temptation should be firmly resisted. Etymologically, *expert* means "one who has experienced," and *amateur* means "one who loves." These are not exclusive categories. Members of faith communities are both experts and amateurs in the kind of social analysis they are called upon to practice. This does not mean that specialists cannot be helpful. They are often valuable resource persons, providing empirical and analytical content, disabusing the group of certain stereotypes, but especially modelling this theological behavior of social analysis. Hence, as a group calls upon some well-chosen specialist for assistance, it is imperative that it keep the primary responsibility for what it is doing, and the basic confidence that it can do it well enough to further its own pastoral purpose.

3. Theological Reflection

Now comes a second shift of mood and climate as we move further around the pastoral circle to the phase of theological reflection. Here again it is important to be free and flexible in the different phases of a process that is organically one. My general conception of theological reflection is that:

1) It exercises itself on the chosen societal situation which has been both experienced and analyzed;

2) It has a twofold function within the pastoral circle:

     a) it is *evaluative*, that is, it makes judgments based on the Gospel, naming the societal situation or specific elements in it as sinful and/or graced;

     b) it is *suggestive*, that is, on the basis of the Gospel it envisages some broad alternatives to the present, alternatives which are also sinful and/or graced, with a view to future decision.

Let me enlarge on each of these roles of theological reflection. As *evaluation*, theological reflection in this restricted sense measures the societal context by the standards of the Gospel. It pronounces judgment, it takes a stand, by saying, "This is a sinful situation," or "This is a graced institution," or "This particular situation is a mixed bag of darkness and light, sin and grace." Its evaluations will be more specific than this, of course. It will say, for instance, "It is not right that in our city hundreds of the poor sleep in the streets while thousands of the affluent enjoy excessive comfort and security in their condominiums." Or, "The tax structure of our nation (or state) is unfairly tilted towards the affluent or towards large corporations." Or, "Women are unfairly dealt with in the administrative structure of our diocese." Or, "Family life in our parish is basically healthy, but is increasingly being threatened by the following cultural influences."

Such an evaluation needs to be based on some norm or

"ought." What is that "ought"? It may generally be described as "the Gospel." More concretely, the norms for evaluating societal situations as sinful and/or graced will be drawn from: 1) the Scriptures, especially the New Testament; and 2) the Church tradition touching the morality of life in society, especially as that tradition has been richly formulated in the social doctrine on the Church in the past century. One might also add the less strictly normative resources of contemporary social theology and philosophy, which can be very helpful in mediating the two basic norms. From all three of these sources, each of which has a very distinctive role, groups engaged in theological reflection will derive the insights and convictions which make possible informed moral judgments, which are both sound and firm.

This is not the place for a disquisition on methodology. Somehow, in a way suited to this way in theology, Scripture, the Church's social teaching, and the refinement of both on the part of social theologians, need to enlighten specific social situations so as to yield the evaluative judgments necessary for effective action. Certain things are obvious — for example, that literalism and fundamentalism are to be avoided in the interpretation of Scripture and tradition; that the hermeneutical process is not linear or dedutive or one-directional; that a sound evaluation is interdependent with the quality of the experiential story and of the social analysis which has preceded it. Beyond that, while acknowledging that complexity besets every step taken around the pastoral circle (so that there is room for enlisting the help of professional theologians), I would insist that, within this new way in theology, basic communities have within themselves the resources for judging societal situations on the basis of the Gospel. The goal is not a significant advance in theological scholarship, but action — a pastoral praxis which is reciprocal with the other phases of the process.

As *suggestion*, that is, as envisaging alternatives to the present, this phase of the circle is a work of theological imagination. The primary service rendered by this exercise is to let the community become an agent of Christian hope, which, especially in the face of impasse and despair, draws on the power and prom-

ise of God in order to envisage and promote a brighter future. "I
know the plans I have in mind for you — it is Yahweh who
speaks — plans for peace, not disaster, reserving a future full of
hope for you" (Jeremiah 29:11). In transcendent terms this
dreamed-of future is heaven, the consummation of the Kingdom
of God. But Christian hope also generates dreams of justice and
peace within history. The pioneers of the anti-slavery struggle a
few centuries ago refused to acquiesce in the inevitability of
slavery. Similarly, the feminist movement today, on the basis of
Gospel values, dreams of a world in which women and men are
not diminished by an unjust exclusion of women from certain
roles. Hence, under the aegis of theological reflection we place
not only the theological evaluation of the sinful present but also
the theological suggestion of a graced future.

In a secondary but important manner, theological imagination will see to it that the reflecting community keeps present to
the possibility of the escalation of societal sin to even more demonic proportions. Our culture, wedded to the Hollywood happy
ending, gives a hard time to any view of the future that is not
optimistic. It is quick to tag such views as doomsaying and Cas-
sandra-like. But prophets like Jeremiah and Amos have taught
us to be wary of crying, "Peace, peace" when there is no peace in
the making. The fear generated by somber analyses and evaluations of the present need not be paralyzing or enervating; integrated with grief and anger, it can generate the kind of courage
needed for a deepening of commitment to a better future.

As one looks at these two exercises of theological reflection,
evaluation and suggestion, recourse to the Jungian functions
can once again be helpful. What is primarily at work in evaluation is the feeling function, whose role is precisely to bring basic
values to bear on situations calling for judgment and decision.
The thinking function will also be involved, since Gospel values
need to be embodied in rational principles of justice if they are to
be fully operative. The other role of theological reflection,
suggesting alternatives, draws on the intuiting function.
Theological imagination, so widely discussed by professional
theologians today, exercises itself in part by providing alterna-

tives to an oppressive present. Walter Brueggemann, in *The Prophetic Imagination*, eloquently describes the dynamic of the prophetic movement as it deals with situations of impasse and numbness. The prophetic community is in a sense fulfilling a priestly role when it summons itself and the wider Church back to fidelity to a neglected heritage; in this respect the feeling function is exercised as the community retells its story and finds again its values. But this recall feeds into what is primary in the prophetic charism, namely the generation of dreaming hope in a despairing or distracted people through the proposal of a graced alternative future. It is true that the prophetic community may also be the bearer of divine threat, or impending doom., Fear that evil may be enlarged has an important place in the dynamic of social change. But the principal role of theological reflection as prophetic is to enlarge the horizon of hope, and to set loose creative energies in a way that will foster the holy decisions of a truly Christian discernment.

4. Pastoral Decision

Holy decision and action bring the pastoral circle to completion, and to fresh beginning. The reflecting community is being asked not merely to evaluate its context and to envisage what might be a better context, but also to take practical steps to change its context and, more importantly, to transform itself for the better in the changing context. Several remarks about this decisional phase are in order.

First, pastoral decision does involve transformation of the community even more than transformation of the context. About a decade ago, I heard Fr. William Fraser of Maryknoll give a lucid presentation of how different modern thinkers have approached the question of where evil comes from and how it is to be combated. Thinkers like Rousseau and Marx have tended to situate the source of our woes in society. Freud and many others who have focused on the psychological limitations of the individual tend, on the other hand, to accent the need for people to be healed before society is healed. About the same time as Bill Fraser's talk, Peter Henriot wrote in *Soundings* that only a "principle of simultaneity" was adequate for grasping how human and Christian transformation takes place. Persons and communities will be transformed towards justice and peace only by engaging in the struggle to establish peace and justice in the world.

When we realize that structures and institutions, society and culture, are not mere *things*, separate from individuals and communities, but rather are the societal actualization or embodiment of persons and communities, they are seen to be realities of human consciousness — and of the human unconscious — as well as objective human creations. No human behavior in the world leaves the human subject unchanged. Our faith decisions must be seen as having both an objective and a subjective pole. These are distinct, to be sure, and not necessarily of equal quality from a moral and religious point of view. A holy personal deed is not by the fact of its holiness a healthy socializing of the Gospel. Even saints, through their cultural limitations, can share and spawn dehumanizing ideologies; on the other side, the flawed action of sinners can be creative of societal blessings. Still, the goal of Christian decision and action needs always, simultaneously, to include both the transformation of society and the continuing conversion of the acting community.

In more traditional terms we may say that Christian decision is an act of prudence, not merely of art. This distinction helps to provide a rationale for insisting on the inseparability of subject and object in virtuous social action. The quality of what we might term societal or political art is to be judged purely from the societal effect, whereas the quality of prudent societal action is also to be judged by what happens to the acting subject. A dramatic example of this occurred as I was writing this chapter. At one point of the effort of the *Agape* community in the Northwest to stop "the white train," which carries nuclear warheads from Texas to the state of Washington, the protesters resorted to tactics which, for James Douglass, were not compatible with the philosophy of non-violent action. Deeply grieved by what had happened to the crowd so intent on winning a skirmish, he pleaded guilty to the charge brought against the violators. In a remarkably eloquent statement, Douglass pointed out that when our resistance to "the white train," symbol of nuclear violence, brings us to any kind of violence ourselves, we become "the white train."

The point is worth lingering with, because a reflecting community can go astray in two opposite directions. It can become so enamoured of success in effecting social change that it loses its soul, through violence or burnout or some other inner contradiction. Or it can become solipsistic, preoccupied with its own spiritual progress, and out of touch with whether it is transforming life around it. It is important that the method followed in the pastoral circle be one which fosters the simultaneous transformation of the community and of its milieu.

Once it is clear that pastoral decision has this dual character, we may go on to approach it from the standpoint of the communal discernment of spirits. Here we touch on what was said in Chapter 5 on the Ignatian approach to Christian decision. Recalling what we said there about the need for liberation from both illusion and addiction, we are helped to understand the basic conditions for faithful pastoral decision.

It is all too clear to anyone who has been part of a group commitment around some social issue that we all bring to discussion a heavy baggage of misperception and fixation. The first draft of this chapter is being written in the final week of the 1984 presidential campaign. The circles within which I discuss the various issues contain, for the most part, people who will vote as I will. A broad consensus on the parties and the candidates exists. Yet when I listen to myself and others speak of these issues I detect that in large part we perceive what we are conditioned by our cultural setting to perceive; we tend to close ourselves from learning from the adversary; and we speak as if any reasonable person ought to vote as we do. We may well be right, at least in general, in our political conclusions and practice. But if in the process of arriving at those conclusions we have engaged in a decisional process of poor quality, then we have added to the smog which darkens and pollutes common political discourse in our land.

Genuine pastoral decision, in contrast, will proceed with a wariness towards knee-jerk political evaluations. Communities which are serious about improving the quality of social and political action will build in appropriate times and spaces for prayer and reflection, aimed at unveiling and neutralizing the mental blocks and emotional fixations which impede holy decision. Such discernment techniques as calling the entire group to argue first against the proposal being considered and then, after time for individual prayer and reflection, to argue in favor of it, can be helpful for enlarging the freedom of the participants.

Besides recourse to spiritual and devotional ways of enhancing a community's understanding and freedom, a discerning use of secular learning about decision making is advisable. Recent decades have provided an almost endless array of helps for individuals and groups. These tools either remotely or proximately can dispose both individuals and groups to move in a more human and authentic way in making choices. They can help us, for example, to improve our ability to listen to each other, to signal to one another that we are indeed listening, to respect the diverse rhythms and preferences of different personality types, to call forth one another's distinctive contributions, to be assertive but not aggressive, and to deal creatively with conflict, ennue, and turmoil.

Some of these techniques have the special value of enabling a group to proceed to decision and implementation in an orderly fashion. "Management by objectives" is one familiar phrase referring to such techniques. With varying degrees of formal structure, it is important for pastoral communities to set goals and objectives, to elaborate policies and programs, to assign responsibility and provide for accountability, to fix budgets, to build in periodic evaluations of performance, and so forth. Discretion is needed, of course, lest David be encumbered by the armor of Saul. A ministry team in a small country parish and the senate of a large archdiocese will not proceed with the same structures and formalities. But experience shows that a good many groups, highly intuitive and feeling in their gifts, need the discipline that comes from the sensing function in its empirical skills, and from the thinking function as it provides adequate structures for difficult endeavors.

That being said, I must at once add that pastoral decision needs to be closely integrated with the other phases of the circle; that it must retain flexibility and creativity if it is to be a true discernment in the Spirit; and that, in the long run, it calls on all four of the Jungian functions. For example, let us suppose that an important and difficult choice keeps being blocked by intangible forces at work in the group. The reasons pro and con may be quite clear, and it might appear that the time has come to make the decision. But though the matter be quite clear, the group may not be at peace within itself. This may well be a moment for disengaging from the immediate decisional process in order to engage in individual and/or communal prayer, or to bring the process back to the level of story or symbol or dream. There is a time for everything in communal discernment, and sensitivity to what it is time for *now* is an indispensable factor in holy decision. Sometimes it can be helpful to a group to have one or more members assigned to listen and observe how the energy is flowing, so that at moments of impasse or confusion they may suggest moving to another point on the pastoral circle. I have also heard of a group which has a member silently praying at all times as those around her participate more articulately in the process.

Friendship/Society and the Circle

In the course of this description of how the pastoral circle works there has been occasion to note how the Jungian model can be helpfully brought to bear on the process. I have also attended to some of the points made in the chapter on the Ignatian exercises — notably the importance of the group being disposed for what it is doing at each phase of the circle, and the relevance of what has been said about the discernment of spirits. Let me now add a final word on the Walden model as it relates to the process. The primary agent of this new way in theology, we have seen, is the group, and so it is the second term in the Walden model, friendship, which is most relevant to this exercise. This is preeminently a "we" theology. But the Walden model will remind us that the enlightenment and freedom of the group is contingent on the enlightenment and freedom of its single members. It also reminds us of the need for spaces and times of solitude, needed by all but especially by introverts who might be undone by too much unrelieved interaction with others.

The societal dimension is likewise relevant to theologizing with the help of the pastoral circle. For one thing, the group itself will generate its own societal and cultural climates, which in turn will impact on each person and on the group as a whole. Because, too, the typical agenda for pastoral reflection is some aspect of life in the larger Church or in society, the group will always be called to be sensitive to the structures and institutions, sinful and graced, which impede or foster an integral life of faith. This sensitivity will find its peak expression in the phase of social analysis, but it will also be important at the stage of pastoral decision, especially if this involves a choice to modify, abandon, or invent some important pastoral structure.

If, as many believe, the grass roots community is the key to the future of the Christian mission, then sound method in the workings of the community is key to its power. And the method is the message; that is, the community will already be saying to itself and to others by the quality of its decision making processes that it stands on the side of human dignity and an integral understanding of the human. The pastoral circle offers to such budding communities a particular method worth trying.

Questions for Reflection

For personal spirituality:

1. Though the pastoral circle is offered primarily for group processes, can I learn from it how to make important personal decisions?

For ministry:

1. Does your pastoral team, and your living community, have an identifiable process or method of making ordinary or extraordinary decisions?

2. Which of the phases of the pastoral circle seem more difficult for your group as a whole, and for individual members? Are you inclined to overdo, or underdo, one or another phase?

3. When your group is engaged in reflection, are you sensitive to how the energy is flowing, to the obstacles to a healthy flow, and to the effective steps to be taken to deal with the obstacles?

11
Cultural Evangelization

The final chapter of this book relates to the most recent stage of my personal theological journey, and represents the principal way in which I currently name the mystery of Christ. Here my chief benefactor has been Joe Holland, mentioned in the previous chapter and elsewhere in this book. When I moved to the Woodstock Theological Center in 1977, I quickly learned to appreciate the intuitive yet disciplined way in which Joe's pastoral mind worked. I remember hearing him speak in those days of two distinct currents within twentieth century Marxism: a rationalistic current represented by the French Marxist, Louis Althusser, and another current, more positive in its appraisal of the role of culture and religion, associated with Antonio Gramsci, the Italian Communist. Something in me resonated with this distinction, and I quickly recognized a broad affinity between what Joe was saying and the accent on transrational dimensions of human processes which I had picked up from fellow Jesuit George Wilson and his associates at Management Design, Inc. (MDI). As Joe began to speak and write of three distinctive responses of the Catholic Church to industrialization, utilizing in this endeavor the analysis of root metaphors done by Gibson Winter, I found myself even more attracted to his schema. He participated in a WTC project directed by me, and his essay for the project appeared in 1982 in the volume edited by Jim Hug, *Tracing the Spirit*.[1]

And so, rather suddenly, I found myself in the late seventies thinking not only in terms of faith and justice, societal sin and societal grace, and the Walden model for linking personal, interpersonal, and societal reality; but in terms of the growing conviction that culture, as the matrix of political, economic, and social structures, was *the* key determinant of the flow of human energies, and therefore the crucial mediation between Christian faith and human society.

Other engagements and contacts of those years nourished this interest in culture and inculturation. At the Woodstock Center I met Marcello Azevedo, a Brazilian Jesuit who had recently completed advance studies at the New School in New York. His was a very scholarly approach to the issue which now intrigued me. A dense paper presented by him in Jerusalem and Rome, subsequently modified for publication, provided further assurance that I was on the right track.[2] So did exposure to several other Jesuits during those same Washington years. Each of the members of the *The Context of Our Ministries* project, undertaken on behalf of our U.S. Provincials, contributed to my enlightenment, including: Peter Henriot, whose collaboration with Joe Holland I have already mentioned; Joe Fitzpatrick, whose essay on faith and culture in our volume reflected decades of sociological research and ministry with Puerto Ricans in New York City; Edmundo Rodriguez, a real embodiment of the Hispanic culture in our Southwest; John Coleman, whose subsequent book, *An American Strategic Theology*, contains dense and relevant treasures; and John Kavanaugh, who in our meetings, as in his *Following Christ in the Consumer Society*, provided an enlightened countercultural challenge.[3] I was fortunate, too, at the Religious Formation Conference meeting in Pittsburgh in the fall of 1981, to be exposed to more brilliance in the shape of Jesuit John Staudenmeier's reflections on the linkage between technology, culture, and religious life.

This kind of education led me to listen to the U.S. Bishops' pastoral on peace with ears attuned to the cultural implications of the challenge they were addressing to us. Around that time I stumbled across Paul VI's Apostolic Exhortation, *Evangelization in the World of Today*, written in 1975, and was thrilled with some of his powerful statements on the evangelization of culture(s). Thus it came about that, in a workshop at Fordham in 1982 and in a lecture under the auspices of the Intercommunity Center for Justice and Peace in the spring of 1984, and eventually in an article in *America* in June, 1984, I dealt with the

peace pastoral from the standpoint of cultural evangelization.[4]
I also had occasion to contribute to LCWR and CMSM dialogues
in recent years essays on religious life which adapted Joe Holland's three root metaphors to describe three very different
kinds of language in use today regarding religious life.[5] And so,
as this book moves towards its conclusion, culture and inculturation represent the primary area for my reading, writing, and
speaking. The following reflections sketch out a model expressive of the conviction that cultural evangelization is at the heart
of the Church's spiritual and pastoral endeavors today.

Culture in the Church and the World

Christian faith exists only as inculturated, that is, only as em-
bodying and expressing itself in the vehicles and representa-
tions of some particular human culture or complexus of cultures. This commonly accepted — and almost as commonly neglected — truth has its basis in the truth that persons and groups
exist only as affected by culture. Nothing human is acultural. If
the Word was made flesh in our humanity, then the flesh of the
Word is not only human, material, societal, but also cultural. Incarnation and inculturation are two ways of naming the same
mystery, and of naming the same foundation for all true
evangelization.

The challenge of inculturation is a challenge for ecclesiology,
which today seeks to deepen its grasp of the Church/culture relationship. If the Church is both communion of believers and
mission to the world, it must continually deal with the question
of culture within two interwoven patterns of its life, one domestic and one evangelizing. In the present stage of the post-Vatican II era, the Roman Catholic Church grapples with a twofold
question of self-understanding: First, how is the Church called
by the Spirit to relate to the dominant technological culture
which increasingly shapes global consciousness and global
structures? Second, in responding to the first question, what
root metaphor discloses to the Church its cultural identity in
this age? In dealing with the first question we are playing with
the model of evangelization of culture. In dealing with the sec-

ond we are playing with a model suggested by the paradigm of three root metaphors developed by Gibson Winter and Joe Holland. Since the Church is inseparably a missionary community, simultaneously gathered into God's reign, the questions dwell nations may be gathered into God's reign, the questions dwell within each other. Clarity and order suggest that they be handled separately. And a preliminary word regarding culture is needed.

Culture is a term with many definitions and no definition. From the rather amorphous notion of culture as learned behavior to the understanding of culture as symbolic expression of human meanings and values, proposed definitions of culture cover a wide range. Here I will attempt not a definition but a description which might be compared to our circling slowly around a sculpture, describing as we go what strikes us. First, culture has to do with meanings and values, which are both discovered and created by the characteristic workings of the human spirit in its deeper penetrations into life. Second, culture resides both in human consciousness and the human unconscious, on the one hand, and in various social embodiments which express and in turn shape our consciousness/unconscious. Third, culture is a communal and societal heritage, and serves as the matrix of the structures and institutions which define social, political, and economic life. Fourth, religious faith is both immanent in culture as in a matrix and yet transcendent to all other facets of culture such as art or philosophy; it is concerned with ultimate meanings and values and its distinctive character is to link the totality of the inculturated human with the Absolute. Fifth, culture for our present purpose is viewed in relationship to four basic human capacities or faculties: basic reason, mythic memory, symbolic and dreaming imagination, and affective commitment. Each of these, in its resonance with the unconscious life of a cultural group, contains distinctive energies for shaping the attitudes and forms of society.

When we speak of cultures and structures, then — whether these be racial, national, or religious, or based on age or sex or economic status — we are dealing with climates of life which are

deeper, more powerful, and more difficult to change and direct
than political and economic structures as such. Culture contains primary energy and resiliency because, through such factors as heritage and tradition, Utopian vision, steadfast loyalty,
and the articulation of credal principles — all of which feed into
and are fed by myth and symbol — they engage the communal
understanding and freedom of human beings more powerfully
than sheer economic necessity or political expediency. Not by
bread alone do humans live, unless and until "bread" achieves a
mythic/symbolic status (as in "bread and roses" or "bread and
wine").

Technological Culture

Such a working definition of culture enables us to grasp what
is meant by speaking in general terms of technological culture.
Technology in the modern sense, rooted in the scientific, industrial, and technical breakthroughs of recent centuries, has obviously affected our political, economic, and social life in unprecedented ways. It has thereby impacted on the various cultures
and subcultures which lie beneath such structures. What is
even more significant is the way in which, within Western society and even within the Third World, technology in its interaction with a given cultural reality has tended to generate a culture of its own, one that bears its image and obeys its inner laws,
and so tends to transform its human objects into "technological
man." The complex dynamic by which the life of basic rationality, mythic memory, dreaming and symbolic imagination, and
affective commitment become instruments of the technological
society is constituted especially by the utilization of the media
of communication, and more broadly by the entry of technology
into the patterns of primary human experience, eating and
drinking, marrying and raising a family, buying and selling,
travelling, making a home, getting educated, enjoying leisure,
engaging in work or profession, and so forth.

One does not have to be a Luddite, or even a disciple of Jacques Ellul in his dour prognostications, to be apprehensive

about the impact of the technological culture on human and Christian values. In a Gospel perspective, technology represents a special gift, the extension of the human response to God's call to be responsible stewards of the whole creation. Particular technological advances have certainly been put on the side of what is human. Many, including the present writer, who are critical of the technological culture, would not be alive and capable of such criticism were it not for having benefited from medical technology. Still, for a variety of reasons, this powerful new culture is massively threatening human awareness and human freedom.

When it becomes an instrument of the prevailing ideology of advanced capitalistic society, technology serves the interests of the directing powers of that society, especially through the promotion of consumerism and elitism. The allure of the comfortable life and the promise of alleviating some basic anxieties — about security, intimacy, social acceptance, and the like — are the lures with which this culture hooks people from nursery to wheel chair. The values symbolized by flag, family, and faith become instrumentalized through a powerful kerygma and catechesis. Allied to the civil religion (especially as this makes Russian communism the "focus of evil" in the universe), the linkages between giant corporations, the military and political establishment, and centers for research and policy formation constitute a powerful triad whose influence is strategically exerted not primarily in the halls of Congress but in advertising and forms of entertainment, in music and fashion styles, in the subtle encouragement of chemical dependency, and in scores of other cultural forms. The latest "rock" or "punk" album, the advertisements in the *New Yorker* magazine (once so distinctive but now finding counterparts in other periodicals), condominium advertising, the layout of shopping malls, the enticements to enlist in the military (with "Be All You Can Be" as a recent version of the once so simple "Uncle Sam Wants You"), the gentrification of central cities, the lure of travel packages, the rituals of the corporate culture — these are a mere handful of the arenas where people's attitudes and habits are most powerfully shaped.

What is most daunting in all this is not that one or other human value is assaulted, as abortion, capital punishment, neglect of the homeless, and persecution of refugees become stark challenges. It is rather the numbing of moral and religious sensibility, the contraction of inner freedom, and the acceleration of societal despair of living in a truly human way. The culture of technologism pollutes the very wellsprings of awareness and freedom, the sources of the indignation and courage without which specific political, economic, and social issues will not be effectively faced.

Evangelizing Culture

The critical area for evangelization, then, is not political and economic life but their cultural matrix; not the pragmatic processes of public life but the forces which play with the basic human endowments of basic reason, mythic memory, symbolic and dreaming imagination, and affective commitment. What puts human energies on the side of life or of death is primarily the quality of our grasp of basic meaning, the quality of story and remembrance, the quality of dreaming and imaging alternatives to the present, and the quality of deep commitment to human values. My contention is that these primordial gifts are being powerfully manipulated by the prevailing forces of the consumer culture, and are in that manipulation being trivialized and stripped of their power to render life more human.

As I have already indicated, confirmation for this accent on the importance of culture for the Church's mission comes from Paul VI's Apostolic Exhortation, *On Evangelization in the Modern World.*[6]

> It is a question not only of preaching the Gospel in ever wider geographic areas or to ever greater numbers of people but also of affecting and as it were upsetting, through the power of the Gospel, humankind's criteria of judgment, determining values, points of interest, lines of thought, sources of inspira-

tion and models of life, which are in contrast with the
word of God and the plan of salvation. (n.19)

And again:

> What matters is to evangelize human culture and
> cultures, not in a purely decorative way, as it were,
> by applying a thin veneer, but in a vital way, in depth,
> and right to their very roots. (n. 20)

In the past few decades, both in theology and in pastoral practice, the U. S. Church has been progressively moving from a
privatized understanding of the Gospel to one that recognizes
its political character. Out of such a realization have come initiatives such as the pastoral letters on peace and the economy,
such organizations as *Network* and the *Center of Concern*, and
such communities as *Sojourners*. Such a conversion is by no
means universal in the U. S. Church, and there is continuing
need to educate Catholics to understand that their faith and religious practice do not stop at the threshold of political and
economic life. But even as this deprivatizing effort continues, its
pioneers are being asked to take a further step, namely to acknowledge that their efforts in the political and economic sectors are doomed to frustration unless they deal effectively with
the rootedness of these sectors in cultural attitudes and habits.
Political and economic ministries remain important expressions
of cultural evangelization, but they are neither unique nor isolated from other thrusts which aim more directly at the cultural
roots of our current malaise.

What makes this model of evangelization more congruous is
the fact that the Church itself exists only as inculturated, and
that the most powerful mediations of the Gospel at its disposal
are cultural in nature. As Christopher Dawson said long ago,
religion is at the heart of culture. Culture — inculturation — is
a comprehensive term for describing what the Church's mission
and ministry are all about. Because the Church experiences and
proclaims the presence of the transcendent mystery within

human life, the carriers of its mission are coextensive with the human. Basic reason, mythic memory, symbolic and dreaming imagination, and affective commitment, are powerfully engaged through the sacramentality which permeates every facet of ministry. In ritual, song, homily, catechesis, the same story is told over and over again; the senses are engaged; the sensible gestures and movements become symbols pointing beyond themselves; the search through the word for the language of faith yields a firmer grasp on meaning, and evokes dreams of another world as well as of a better this-world; and in vocational sacraments, religious vows, and other public vowing, deep affective commitment is called forth. The most enduring carriers of the Church in history are not hierarchical structure or theological elaborations of the mystery but popular devotion, contemplative practice, the daily routines of the corporal and spiritual works of mercy — a total corporate life of faith that has found appropriate cultural embodiment.

But also inappropriate cultural embodiment. That inculturation has its shadow side goes without saying, in a Church which shares in the sin/grace dialectic: sacramentalism and superstition; captivity to the prevailing secular culture; or at the other extreme the burgeoning of narrow and defensive ecclesiastical cultures alienated from the lives of ordinary people. H. Richard Niebuhr's classic *Christ and Culture* has rung the changes on the historical stances taken by the Church in response to the surrounding cultures. Paul Tillich set his whole theology within the framework of particular cultures providing the forms of the perennial question of ultimate concern to which the Church seeks to respond on the basis of the Gospel.

Reaching Global Culture Today

Here, then, is a partial response to our first question: How is the Church called by the Spirit of Christ to relate to the dominant technological culture which increasingly shapes global consciousness and global structures? My response is that the primary target of the Church's evangelization needs to be the technological culture itself, not just the political and economic structures which institutionalize that culture. And, secondly, I am saying that in this endeavor the Church needs to draw principally on its cultural resources; that is, on renewed and adapted vehicles of basic reason, mythic memory, symbolic and dreaming imagination, and affective commitment. Someone has described the present encounter of Christianity and technological culture as a clash of two faiths, each with its own creed, ritual, code, and its own catechumenate. With consummate skill the technological culture knows how to initiate new members, beginning with pre-nursery tots. Through logo and ditty, through tunes and fashions, through the clever appropriation of deep patriotic or ethnic or familial or other nostalgic and Utopian energies, it turns out, around the world, devotees of the consumer way of life. The challenge put to the community of disciples of Jesus is to withstand this contemporary embodiment of the principalities and powers, and to offer experiences of initiation and ongoing formation in the Gospel which humanize instead of dehumanizing the flow of human energy.

In the watershed of the post-Vatican II experience, the various Christian churches have been struggling with this challenge, with results that are mixed and still ambiguous. One of the factors contributing to widespread confusion has been the lack of any clear cultural identity on the part of Church members, or rather, the lack of the clear realization that the transition and the crisis they are enduring is basically a cultural one. The present situation calls for a recasting, in cultural terms, of the problem of fidelity spoken of in Chapter 6: How are we to find and sustain a way of life, that is, a viable cultural embodiment of the Gospel, that is both tenacious of the once for all Word of God spoken into our midst and at the same time open to the present movement of the unpredictable Spirit of God? Because the present movement of the Spirit deals with the confrontation of Christianity and the technological culture, this brings us to the second question of this chapter: What is the root metaphor which discloses to the Church its cultural identity in this technological age?

Root Metaphors for Today

As already noted, I have derived a good deal of light on this question from Joe Holland's application of the three root metaphors described by Gibson Winter to three stages of the Church's response to industrialization and, more broadly, to modernization and the secularization of Western society. Here, then, is a final model: the organistic, mechanistic, and artistic root metaphors which can serve as interpretive and evaluative tools on behalf of the Church's evangelization of U.S. and world culture. What follows is my own rather simplified rendition of what Winter and Holland have elaborated with greater nuance and density.

The term "root metaphor" I take to point to a way or level of knowledge more iconic or imaged than conceptual. It suggests that beneath various analytical models and paradigms lie more amorphous gatherings of psychic energy which obscurely but powerfully shape the workings of pragmatic reason and technical efficiency. Hence the appropriateness of the term *metaphor*. Second, we are dealing with *root* metaphors. Some of these gatherings of psychic energy are so primordial and so comprehensive that they constitute, as it were, the hidden horizon or *Denkform* which permeates more specific metaphors and their resultant concepts and terms. One may, for example, use a term like "authority" or "obedience" within each of the three root metaphors I will be describing. But in each case the term is mediating a meaning which can be fully grasped only within that root metaphor.

Both a Roman canonist and an American woman religious may use words like "obedience" and "authority" in expressing some enduring ecclesial value. But if the former is working on the basis of an organicist root metaphor and the latter on the basis of a mechanistic or artistic root metaphor, what is being communicated will be profoundly different. The challenge of dialogue for such participants lies not so much in their not being able to agree on certain propositions as in their finding it extremely difficult to grasp the deeper connotations of the terms in the mind of the dialogue partner.

A further characteristic of the root metaphors is that they

have been formed out of some dominant cultural experience which has affected every facet of life within that culture. The first root metaphor, for example, is designated as organicist because the society in which it developed experienced life predominantly within the organic cycles, the recurring rhythms of nature as then understood. Without attempting historical validation, let me name several key conceptual expressions of this first metaphor: order, objective certitude, hierarchy, sacrality. These will be recognized as characteristic traits of the Gospel's feudal and medieval inculturation. For centuries medieval Christendom lived the Gospel through ideas, practices, dogmas, codes, rituals, and pervasive habits of life which accented the importance of law and order; clarity in doctrinal and moral formulations; careful distinction between the spiritual and the temporal together with an insistence on the superiority of the former over the latter; and the primacy of the common good over the good of individuals.

The dominant experience which originated the second root metaphor, the *mechanistic* one, was the industrial revolution or the coming of the "machine age." Tilling the soil and working on an assembly line are sharply different experiences (the all but complete conquest of the family farm by agribusiness in our country dramatizes this conquest). Especially when taken together with culturally congruous political, economic, and social revolutions, the industrial revolution brought Western society to a new way of dealing with life. A list of the notable conceptual expressions of the second root metaphor would include, among others, historicity and subjectivity; the cherishing of doubt in the search for truth; focus on the individual as subject of rights and responsibilities; the privatizing of religion, together with the secularization of political, economic, and social values and structures; democratization. The contrast of these first two mindsets is clear, and could be analyzed at considerable length.

Winter and Holland in fact view our contemporary crisis from the perspective of the clash between these two root metaphors and their ideological and institutional corollaries. Both see the hope of resolution of the crisis in a third root metaphor, designated as *artistic*. As the creation of art constitutes a less tangible phenomenon than the tilling of the soil or the working of a machine, so the elucidation of this third root metaphor will seem necessarily nebulous by comparison, especially because its historical embodiment is still in the making. Among the terms which give it some voice I would include: a holistic sense of life; process and relationship rather than substance; discernment; solidarity (non-organic communion). I would see some of the key insights of the feminist, ecological, and non-violence movements as instancing the emergence of this third root metaphor. It would appear that the new physics, especially when it speaks in a language akin to mysticism, is moving from the second towards the third way of viewing life.

The notion of dialectic may be helpful in conceiving the relationship between the three root metaphors, the artistic serving as the synthetic transcending of impasse between the first and second metaphors. Where, for example, the modern movement into subjectivity, historicity, and respect for the individual paid for its advance in the spawning of individualism, the retrieval within the third root metaphor of a stronger sense of wholeness and the common good represents not a return to an organicist model but a movement forward to a new holistic view of life. Another important example: in deprivatizing modernity's relegation of the role of religious faith, the third root metaphor would not be content with merely reinstating the medieval sacral/secular domination model, but would look for ways to endorse, while transcending, the gains of modernity regarding the "autonomy" of secular process.

Joe Holland throws light on Church history in the post-Tridentine period when he hypothesizes three successive phases of the Roman Catholic response to industrialization.[7] The first response was negative and defensive, and seemed incapable of accepting that the Gospel was viable other than in medieval and feudal dress. The second response, made gradually and grudgingly, was one of accommodation to modern culture; especially in the past century it has been open to ways of inculturating the Gospel within the forms of modern Western society. The third response, which is as yet a grassroots one, provides energies for what is most radically innovative in Christian movements today.

What has struck me, especially in viewing the tensions presently existing between the Holy See and U.S. women religious, is that all three mentalities coexist in the life of the contemporary Church. The organicist root metaphor and its ideological expressions are by no means dead in the continuing quest for self-definition on the part of the Church. Especially in the face of the risks — and the consequences of the risks taken — inherent in accommodation to the liberal society, the reaffirmation of traditional values has its place, even though its distinctive language and preferred structuring of Church life runs the danger of being reactionary. Whereas, for example, many U.S. religious speak very positively of their place in the world, the new law of the Church speaks of religious life as one separated from the world.

Between the second and third root metaphors, too, there are tensions. Where the former, for example, would encourage a language and a structuring of Church life which accents the autonomy of the individual over against the institution, the latter would shift the emphasis to a new mode of communality, quite different from the hierarchical corporateness congruous with the first root metaphor. In other words, the present tensions and struggles in the life of the Church may be viewed, with the help of the three root metaphors, as occurring on the basis of three cultural approaches among which there is both communality and divergence.

This kind of analysis does not necessarily lead to despair of resolving the tensions or, on the other hand, to a bland blessing of everything without the need of tough decision. It recognizes the limited character of each approach, and it affirms that each is capable of being corrected in some respects by the other two. But it is a model derived from historical analysis, and the movement of history; whatever spiralling it may contain is one-directional — forward to the future. If the model is sound in its histor-

ical analysis, it calls for an option for the third root metaphor
and its consequences. The artistic root metaphor needs to be primary in directing today's evangelization of culture. While continuing to learn from its medieval heritage and from its all too
brief engagement in the liberal society of the West, Christianity
now needs to form itself from such futuristic currents as are contained in feminism, in the new holistic approach to science,
technology, and the care of the planetary environment, and in
non-violence as a way of resolving conflict.

This being said, it calls for some correction in the universal
Church, and even in the U.S. scene. One difficulty with moving
into the mentality of the third root metaphor is that many sectors of the Christian community have hardly assimilated the
values of the second root metaphor. Evangelization and ministry call for ongoing cultural discernment regarding which
values need to be accented in a given situation; which values,
almost necessarily, need to be left unaccented; consequently,
which risks are being chosen; and how the concrete vehicles of
evangelization and ministry are to be employed so as to render
the message authentic and effective. For example, in the struggle to gain in the official Church a more effective recognition of
the rights of women, or of the laity, or of professional theologians, does there not come a point at which both leaders and disciples need to discern within their own attitudes and practice
whether they are speaking and acting from a tired secular
liberalism or from the authentic spirit of the Gospel? It is for this
kind of discernment that the Holy Spirit is continually poured
forth into the hearts of individual believers and into the many
communities of the disciples of Christ.

In summary, then, the contemporary technological culture,
especially where it poses a threat to humankind more radical
than the threat of the arms race or any other single oppression,
needs to be the focus of Christian evangelization. Such evangelization, directed towards culture, is itself inescapably cultural in
expression. It is simply not possible for the word of God to be addressed to any cultural situation without itself being clothed in
a dress which greatly affects the way in which it will engage the

culture. Here is where the typology of Niebuhr's *Christ and Culture* can help us appreciate that the accent, style, and modalities of cultural evangelization must be discerned in every age. It is not to be assumed that the predominant accent in this or that situation will be countercultural, or accommodating, or disengaged, or whatever. Even when, like me, one believes that the artistic root metaphor is to be chosen as basis for evangelization, this leaves open many more specific questions which need to be faced.

Whatever one's biases and options may be, it seems clear that cultural evangelization will be more effective as it draws on the whole panoply of cultural resources within the life of the Church, particularly those which are contemplative, devotional, and sacramental.

Spiritual Liberation

What are some interesting implications of this model for spiritual growth and ministerial practice? Let me respond under three headings.

First, any Christian concerned with personal growth in faith and holiness would do well to attend to the impact of culture on the journey of enlightenment and liberation. The consciousness examen, mentioned in Chapter 2, can profitably be directed to such influences. What forces in family life, in the ethnic or parish or school subcultures in which I grew up, have formed in me through the years identifiable patterns of mythic memory, symbolic and dreaming imagination, and affective commitment? To what extent are these patterns life-giving and freeing, and to what extent do they numb or paralyze my life of faith? For example, have my cultural environments fostered in me healthy attitudes towards authority? Has the mentality of the organicist metaphor tended to make me something of a conformist, accepting unquestionably "whatever Rome says"? Or, have I assimilated from my American cultural milieu such an insistence on individual autonomy and on my personal needs and rights that I am less free to make sacrifices and take risks on behalf of the common good? Or what is the prevailing image that I carry into each day touching my being a man or a woman? Is there some stereotype deriving from a cultural environment which obscures in me the Gospel view of sexuality and the relationship between the sexes? What is that Gospel view; what are the cultural forms in which it expresses itself in my very speaking of it; and do I know how to distinguish in my own enunciation what is enduring and what is not?

This kind of question puts cultural flesh on a basic spiritual challenge which has often been handled too abstractly, the challenge to be progressively freed from "inordinate attachments," "worldly attitudes," and the like.

A more particular exercise would be to test out one's favorite language with the help of the three root metaphors. One might, for example, read a typically Roman description of marriage or religious life; than an author who reflects a liberal point of view; then someone like Johannes Metz on religious life or Rosemary Haughton on marriage and family, beckoning to new ways of conceiving and living our faith. As we read, we can be in touch with the attractions and repugnances which spontaneously occur in us, and discerningly choose with their help what appears to be the language and life style to which God is calling us.

Community Climate

Christian community is a second area where the impact of culture and the call to cultural evangelization may be examined. Whether the community in question is a family, a group of several married couples, a local religious community, a ministerial team, or some parish or campus group, it verifies in some sense and to some degree the idea of a basic community. Now culture of its very nature is a communal possession. The interaction of individuals generates the images, symbols, and patterns of social behavior which are the clues to this or that culture. It is obvious that each and every community carries with it an identifiable cultural climate; that this climate affects persons and relationships; that cultural forces, ecclesial and secular, from outside the community, are continually interacting with energies immanent within the community; and that the whole complex flow of cultural energies is the theatre for the struggle of sin and grace in the world.

A simple consequence of all this is that a community which is truly reflective and discerning will want to include in the scope of its reflection and decisional processes this cultural dimension of life. What common assumptions are at work in the community regarding the sharing of food and drink, conversation, shopping, travel, recreation, hospitality, care of health, and all the other facets of daily life which feel the impact of cultural mindsets? Which influences from surrounding cultures are helpful and which are impeding? To what extent does the community experience a call to be countercultural, even with respect to the Church? Do numbness, paralysis, a latent despair, subtly blunt the sharp call of the Spirit to be a community of prophetic witness? What is the quality of mythic memory, dreaming and symbolic imagination, rational meaning, and affective commitment, as these are exercised within the community and in the projection of its spirit outward? These are some of the questions which need to be asked by any Christian community which has heard the call to engage in the evangelization of culture.

Analysis of Ministerial Situations

Third, regarding ministry I will make one of many possible observations. Each aspect of ministry — sacramental, liturgical, homiletic, catechetical, diaconal — needs to be exercised with sensitivity to the degree and quality of cultural awareness and freedom present in both ministers and those being served. Let us say, for example, that a special effort is being made to communicate to adolescents an understanding of the Church's teaching on peace and economic justice. For such a ministerial effort to become an act of cultural evangelization requires that the ministers be in touch with cultural assumptions. Do Calvin Klein jeans have anything to do with economic justice? Is there any connection between famine in Ethiopia and hanging out at the local Pizza Hut? What are some of the cultural implications of the "Africa Aid" concert of 1985? I am not suggesting here that ministers and the young people share some spasmodic guilt trip. I myself do not have the experience and skills to design the appropriate cultural catechesis for such a ministry. But, along with some rudimentary social, political, and economic analysis, what is crucial is that the hidden cultural barriers to peace and justice be uncovered.

Such cultural discernment leads, as Metz has pointed out, to a revolution that is not merely political or economic but cultural in character. If our U.S. bishops have been brave in challenging us to political and economic conversion, what is the depth of courage needed if the deeper call to cultural conversion is issued to and heeded by all of us in the Church?

Questions for Reflection

For personal spirituality:

1. Let me make an inventory of the points in my ordinary life at which I meet the surrounding technological culture, and try to evaluate the resulting impact on my living of the Gospel.
2. In drawing upon the Christian heritage in my effort to grow, what cultural energies are available to me, and how well do I use them?

For ministry:

1. In analyzing and evaluating the context of our ministry, do I and my associates take cultural factors into consideration?
2. In attending to the group(s) that we serve, which of the three root metaphors seem to be prevalent in attitudes and climates of life?
3. Has our ministerial team discussed its own cultural assumptions, and the ways in which these affect our conduct of ministry?

Epilogue
Continuing to Play

Readers who have persevered to this point will know by now whether this kind of theologizing — linking personal story with reflection — is something that they care to do themselves. In undertaking this book as a kind of ministry, my goal was to foster in others a trust in the validity and value of their own word of faith. Now, after displaying several models and the ways in which they came to me, I wonder whether I myself am not the principal beneficiary of this whole endeavor. The effort has certainly put me back in touch with stages of a journey for which I am grateful, and has renewed my desire to keep travelling. These final few pages are like a scenic overlook on a mountain road. I gaze back at a few other models which, for one reason or another, could not be included here; then I look ahead briefly at what seems to be waiting for me up ahead.

The following retrospective glance may be disconcerting to some readers, since I will be identifying models without developing them or their spiritual and ministerial implications. It turns out that they form something of a cluster, which is chiefly ecclesiological in character.

Representing/Substituting

Dorothee Soelle, in one of her early books, *Christ the Representative*, excited my imagination with a distinction which I have often used in other contexts than the soteriological and "death of God" ones which concerned her in the 1960s. In dealing with our redemption through Jesus Christ and with the "death of God" in our culture, she distinguished between the role of the "substitute" and the role of the "representative." Jesus on the cross truly died for us, but not as a substitute, that is, he did not supplant us, render our engagement superfluous, or otherwise get us "off the hook." Far from making our discipleship a matter of passive acceptance, his provisional standing in the breach for us at a time when we were incapable of standing there ourselves actually calls forth our engagement. And today our call is not to substitute for God but similarly to represent God, provisionally making God present at a period when, in a real sense, he is not able to function.

Though couched in a different language and otherwise focused, this model has much in common with Rahner's understanding of creation as I have outlined it above (Chapter 7). I believe that Soelle's attractive distinction — which is more subtle and profound than I can here convey — may serve as a foundation for distinguishing various roles in the Church. No one in the Church is called to substitute for anyone else, but we are called, in some fashion, to represent in lifestyle or function an aspect of discipleship which is common to all baptized. The hermit, for example, does not get the rest of us off the hook so far as the experience of solitude is concerned; on the contrary, the hermit's representing in public and dramatic fashion this basic aspect of every human and Christian call challenges the rest of us to find, symbolically, our desert, our Mount Athos. It is the same with bishops, priests, contemplative nuns, religious, married people, single people, and those who bear witness to peace and justice through civil disobedience or other forms of dramatic protest. Each of these special callings holds out to all of us a dimension of discipleship which we might otherwise neglect. I find a special value in this model in its power to counteract a substitutionary mentality which is still widespread, and which tends to make priests and religious cultic or prophetic substitutes instead of representatives of the laity of the Church.

Lay/Clerical and Secular/Religious

This ecclesiological model has been fairly close, in my personal reflection, to another model, which deals with different states and roles in the Church. For many years, especially in encountering the pressures exerted by Roman authorities on apostolic women religious, I have been helped by a model that is both theological and canonical. Negatively, this model refuses a concentric circle image of the different groups in the Church, which would put bishops and other clerics at the center, religious further out from the center, and laity on the periphery. Such a model tends to blur the reality of God's call to individual Christians, and also to offer an excuse for undue limitations imposed on the ministry — especially the political ministry — of apostolic religious. Religious who have not been ordained (called "sisters" or "brothers") are not semi-clerics. They belong to the laity of the Church no less than other laity who are not members of religious communities. As the Constitution on the Church of Vatican II says, the religious state is not a middle state between that of clerics and that of the laity; religious life does not belong to the hierarchical structure of the Church (nn. 43-44).

Alternative to the concentric circle model is one which utilizes two traditional theological and canonical distinctions, one between laity and clergy, and the other between seculars and religious. The first of these distinctions has to do with ordained office in the Church, or, we might say, with the distinction between baptismal ordination and the further ordination of some of the baptized through the sacrament of holy orders. As such it does not call for one or other lifestyle; the Latin Church, once again, through the restoration of the permanent diaconate, has married clerics; and marriage is not the only state of life for lay people.

The second distinction, between seculars and religious, does have to do with lifestyle, notably with respect to celibacy or marriage as the modality of Christian chastity. It is perhaps a more risky distinction than the first, for it can miss the wide variety of lifestyles possible for those belonging to one or other of the two groups; and if permitted to carry the medieval connotation of separation from the world as distinctive of religious, it could distort the vocation of apostolic religious. It could be well that this distinction has served its time. While it lasts, however, it can serve, together with the lay/clerical distinction, as a bulwark against the concentric circle model of groupings in the Church.

Institution and Communion

Both of the models just identified, substitution/representation and the distinction of lay/clerical and secular/religious, are pertinent to a third ecclesiological model, derived from a key passage in Vatican II's Constitution on the Church (n. 8). This model distinguishes between the Church as *communion* and the Church as a *structured institution*; like the passage from the Council, it insists that it is the same Church which is both communion and institution; and it accents the fact that the institutional element in the Church is always to be evaluated in its role of fostering communion. What Jesus said about the sabbath being for humans and not vice versa has to be said with respect to hierarchy, law, sacramental system, and every other aspect of the Church as institution. The distinction also provides a base for insisting, with influence from the American experience of voluntarism, that there is a need in the Church for grassroots communities enjoying a larger autonomy than communities and organizations which have been drawn into the immediate workings of the Church as institution. Religious life is a major instance of voluntary, charismatic, grassroots communities called to function within the Church at some distance from the Church's institutional authority. When churchmen become too prone to organizational tidiness this freedom of religious to be prophetic, even and especially within the Church, can be compromised.

A further value of the distinction is expressed in the Constitution on the Church, when it distinguishes between that basic lay apostolate which originates for all in baptism, and the more restricted service of some of the baptized invited to assist the hierarchy in fulfilling its peculiar official role of leadership (n. 33).

Prophet/Civil Servant

A fourth model which I have found helpful is congruous with the first three. In an article in *America* in 1971, I distinguished the role of religious as *prophets* and as *civil servants*.[1] The model is helpful for describing historically what happened to religious (especially women) in the course of U.S. Church history. In effect women religious became the Church's civil servants in staffing the immense parochial school system and other Church institutions. I would not question the wisdom, or the inevitability, of this historical occurrence. But in retrospect, and in consonance with such views as those of Johannes Metz, it is possible to regret a certain domestication of the life of communities whose origins were charismatic and prophetic. Hence, while it makes sense through the prophet/civil servant distinction to signalize the availability of religious for special Church roles, it is important that the prophetic pole of the tension be safeguarded, especially at a period which threatens to absorb religious excessively into the institutional workings of the Church.

Directions for the Future

This brief review of some models not developed in the chapters of this book makes me appreciate that, though I am not an ecclesiologist, much of my reflection has been spent on the different roles and states of people within the Church. And, so far as present conviction is concerned, the development of the call of the laity to holiness and ministry is as close to my heart as any other single issue. Still, when I turn to what kind of model seems to await me further down the road, ecclesiology tends to fade a little. Let me conclude by pointing in a certain direction.

I am fairly certain that culture and the evangelization of culture will continue to intrigue me in the years ahead, and that I will want to move on from what I have set down in Chapter 11. In addition, I have been attracted by the possibilities of the notion of non-violent resistance to evil and conflict resolution, which I see as more comprehensive in its potential than only for the area of peace and justice, where it has been influential up to now. I know that at some point I would like to explore both of these possibilities.

But I am being challenged much more by the little I have read of authors whose context is the material universe and the remarkable leaps being made in understanding it. Something intuitive within me keeps announcing that theological reflection between now and the twenty-first century's beginnings will be centrally concerned with the exploration of space and time from the standpoint of the Gospel, and with the help of an emerging cosmological theology. "Creation-centered spirituality" is perhaps the best known name for this new movement. The phrase is from Matthew Fox, whose writings I have just begun to examine. A profound elaboration of this movement is contained in many unpublished papers of Thomas Berry, who speaks of planetary consciousness and the need for a functional cosmology. Significant and influential for me during the writing of this book was the fact that Joe Holland, whose elaboration of Gibson Winter's three root metaphors had stimulated me so much (as indicated in Chapter 11), has been greatly drawn in similar fashion to build on Thomas Berry's model of four ages of humankind, the tribal, the classical, the scientific-technological, and now the emerging ecological age.

This expansion of the perspective from the cultural to the cosmological has been for me both inviting and startling, both attractive and threatening. Especially where the critique of traditional models has led proponents of this new cosmological theology to call for relinquishment of our basic anthropocentric perspective in favor of a cosmocentric or biocentric one, I am taken aback, even made anxious. As one who was drawn to the vision of Pierre Teilhard de Chardin even before his works were permitted to be published after his death in 1955, I want to be open to even further possibilities of revising previous models. And from reading just a little — and understanding even less — of what physicists and philosophers are saying of our universe, from subatomic energies to astrophysics, I know in principle that strikingly new things remain to be said from the standpoint of the Gospel.

Still, I am anxious. Can the Gospel itself survive what we are learning about the place of humans in this universe of time and space? Does the Gospel not assume an anthropocentric view of the universe, now being questioned in the new cosmology? If there is challenge even in Karl Rahner's suggestion, made not too long before his death, that the Church now enters a third age, an age of truly global consciousness — but still, in Rahner's view, an anthropocentric age — infinitely greater is the challenge now coming from those who have been listening closely not merely to the emerging global village of our earth but to the music of the spheres being heard more clearly through ever more sophisticated technological instruments.

I am drawn, but also anxious. This might seem a strange place to bring these reflections to a close. But anxiety — living with the anxiety of having some basic questions unanswered — can be a powerful source for the energies needed in theological reflection. If it is an anxiety compatible with a faith commitment to the Gospel, or rather, the necessary anxiety inseparable from such a commitment, then it can bear fruit for self and for others. As a graced concern, it can become " . . . my daily preoccupation: my anxiety for all the churches" (2 Corinthians 11:28).

Footnotes

Foreword

[1] I.T. Ramsey, *Models and Mystery*, Oxford University Press, 1964.

[2] J. McIntyre, *The Shape of Christology*, Philadelphia: Westminster, 1966.

[3] A. Dulles, *Models of the Church*, Garden City: Doubleday, 1974.

Chapter 1

[1] H. Adams, *Mont-Saint-Michel and Chartres*, New York: Putnam, 1980.

[2] H. Adams, *Letters to a Niece and Prayer to the Virgin of Chartres*, New York: Houghton Mifflin, 1920.

[3] D. Bonhoeffer, *The Cost of Discipleship*, London: SCM Press, 1948, pp. 37-49.

[4] See the reference to Joanna Macy in the following chapter, note 7.

Chapter 2

[1] "Ignatian Spirituality and Societal Consciousness," *Studies in the Spirituality of Jesuits* 7 (September 1975), No. 1, 127-150.

[2] "Towards Wholeness in Prayer," in: *The Wind is Rising: Prayer Ways for Active People* (ed. W. Callahan and F. Cardman), Hyattsville, MD: Quixote Center, 1978, pp. 18-20.

[3] R. Carignan et al., *Our Search for God as Religious*, Ottawa: *Canadian Religious Conference*, 1984, pp. 83-91.

[4] H. Thoreau, *Walden and Other Writings*, New York: Bantam, 1981, p. 208.

⁵ F. Meehan, *A Contemporary Social Spirituality*, Maryknoll, NY: Orbis, 1982.

⁶ See William Barry's article in *Soundings* (Chapter 2).

⁷ J. Macy, *Despair and Personal Power in the Nuclear Age*, Philadelphia: New Society, 1983.

⁸ See J. & R. Aldridge, "A Nuclear Engineer's Family" in: J. Wallis (ed.), *Peacemakers: Christian Voices from the New Abolitionist Movement*, San Francisco: Harper & Row, 1983, pp. 7-13.

⁹ *Op. cit.*, p. 12.

Chapter 3

¹ They include: "Jungian Types and Forms of Prayer," *Review for Religious* 42 (September-October 1983), No. 5, pp. 661-676; "Jungian Typology and the Gospel Journey," *New Catholic World*, March-April 1984, pp. 86-89.

² See the brief biography in *From Image to Likeness*.

³ The following six paragraphs are taken from the *Review for Religious* article (above, footnote 1).

⁴ *Peace on Earth* n. 167; tr. J. Gremillion, *The Gospel of Peace and Justice*, Maryknoll, NY: Orbis, 1976, p. 238.

⁵ See *From Image to Likeness*, pp. 19-25.

⁶ G. Lawrence, *People Types and Tiger Stripes: A Practical Guide to Learning Styles*, Gainesville, FL: Center for Applications of Psychological Type, 1979.

Chapter 4

¹ "For a Spirituality of Action," *New Catholic World*, July-August 1982, pp. 174-176.

Chapter 5

¹ "The Ignatian Exercises: Contemplation and Discernment," *Review for Religious* 31 (1972) 62-69. The essay was reprinted in my *New Pentecost or New Passion? The Direction of Religious*

Life Today, New York: Paulist, 1973, pp. 156-170.

[2] F. Crowe, "Complacency and Concern in the Thought of St. Thomas," *Theological Studies* 20 (1959) 1-39; 198-230; 343-95; "Complacency and Concern," *Cross and Crown* 11 (1959) 180-190.

[3] See Chapter 2, footnote 1.

[4] "Public Policy and Christian Discernment," in J. Haughey (ed.), *Personal Values in Public Policy: Conversations on Government Decision-Making*, New York: Paulist, 1979, pp. 212-231.

[5] "Jesus at Table: The Ignatian Rules and Human Hunger Today," in: G. Schner (ed.), *Ignatian Spirituality in a Secular Age*, Waterloo, Ontario: Wilfrid Laurier University Press, 1984, pp. 91-112.

[6] *New Pentecost or New Passion?*, p. 168.

Chapter 6

[1] "The Crisis of Permanent Consecration," *Sisters Today* 41 (1969) 1-15.

[2] "Jesuit Commitment — Fraternal Covenant?", *Studies in the Spirituality of Jesuits* 3 (1971) No. 3, pp. 69-101.

[3] H. Arendt, *The Human Condition*, Garden City: Doubleday, 1959, pp. 212-213.

[4] B. Lonergan, "Existenz and Aggiornamento," *Collection*, New York: Herder & Herder, 1967, p. 242; K. Keniston, *The Uncommitted*, Delta, 1965; "Nowhere Man": Copyright 1965, Northern Songs Limited. Used by permission. All rights reserved.

Chapter 7

[1] *Summa Theologica* I, q. 19, a.5.

[2] *Theological Investigations*, vol. 1, New York: Seabury, 1974, p. 162.

[3] London: SCM Press, 1967, p. 196.

[4] *Images of Hope: Imagination as Healer of the Hopeless*, Balti-

more: Helicon, 1965.

[5] J. Milhaven, "Be Like Me! Be Free!", *America* 116 (April 22, 1967) 584-6.

[6] "The Son of the Living God," *The Way* 8 (1968) 97-105.

Chapter 8

[1] The presentation was included in my *New Pentecost or New Passion?*, New York: Paulist, 1973, as Chapter 10, "Freedom Through Dependence," pp. 124-140.

[2] "The Problem of Evil: A New Study," *Theological Studies* 28 (1967) 119-128.

[3] See especially J. Metz, *Faith in History and Society: Towards a Practical Fundamental Theology*, New York: Crossroad, 1980.

Chapter 9

[1] "On the Need to Break Bread Together," in A. Hennelly & J. Langan (eds.), *Human Rights in the Americas: The Struggle for Consensus*, Washington, DC: Georgetown University Press, 1982, pp. 211-244.

[2] See chapter 5, footnote 5.

[3] P. Tillich, *Love, Power, and Justice*, New York: Oxford University Press, 1954; R. Johann, "Love and Justice," in R. de George (ed.), *Ethics and Society: Original Essays on Contemporary Moral Problems*, New York: Doubleday, 1966, pp. 25-47.

[4] "Tender Love, Firm Justice," *The Way* 22, (July 1982) 175-183.

Chapter 10

[1] J. Hug (ed.), *Tracing the Spirit*, New York: Paulist, 1983, p. 34.

[2] *Ibid*, p. 16.

Chapter 11

[1] J. Holland, "Linking Social Analysis and Theological Reflection: The Place of Root Metaphors in Social and Religious Experience," in: J. Hug (ed.), *Tracing the Spirit*, pp. 170-191; see also J. Holland and P. Henriot, *Social Analysis: Linking Faith and Justice*, Maryknoll, NY: Orbis, 1983, pp. 64-86.

[2] M. Azevedo, *Inculturation and the Challenges of Modernity*, Rome: Gregorian University, 1982.

[3] J. Connor et al., *The Context of Our Ministries: Working Papers*, Washington, DC: Jesuit Conference, 1981; J. Coleman, *An American Strategic Theology*, New York: Paulist, 1982; J. Kavanaugh, *Following Christ in a Consumer Society: The Spirituality of Cultural Resistance*, Maryknoll, NY: Orbis, 1981.

[4] "To Make Peace, Evangelize Culture," *America* June 2, 1984, pp. 413-17.

[5] "The Place of Religious Life in the Church: A Theological Reflection," in *LCWR Seminar Papers: Religious Congregations Within the Church*, Washington DC: Leadership Conference of Women Religious, 1982, pp. 1-12; D. Fleming (ed.), *Religious Life at the Crossroads*, New York: Paulist, 1985, pp. 168-189.

[6] Washington DC: U.S. Catholic Conference, 1976, pp. 16-17.

[7] See footnote 1.

Epilogue

[1] "What Are Religious — 'Avant-garde' or Civil Servants?", *America* 25 (October 2, 1971) 232-233.

$8.9

3 5282 00110 3772

"How shall I speak about God and the mystery of human life to myself and to others? What is the language which can best foster conversion and growth in those to whom I minister?" In the past few decades personal and communal reflection on experience has emerged as a powerful source for life-giving speech. A major current in theology serves this process through the generation of appropriate *models*.

Playing in the Gospel offers stimulating examples of how the ordinary Christian's personal history can yield such images and conceptual frameworks. Beginning with the theme of power and energy as found in Jung, Teilhard, and Henry Adams, each chapter tells a personal story of theological insight and then reflects spiritually and pastorally on the resulting model.

The four Jungian functions, Thoreau's "three chairs," action and contemplation, development and liberation, peace and justice, and the "pastoral circle" are among the models which emerge from this exercise of "playing in the Gospel."

These short essays, integrated through the theme of power and energy, aim to further the spiritual growth of all readers and to provide ministers with a helpful reflective language for their service of the Gospel.

Thomas E. Clarke, S.J., is a spiritual and pastoral theologian residing in New York City. He was a professor of systematics at Woodstock College (a Jesuit seminary), and a resident fellow of Woodstock Theological Center at Georgetown University. Among other publications, he is author of *New Pentecost or New Passion?*, co-author of *From Image to Likeness: A Jungian Path in the Gospel Journey,* and editor of *Above Every Name: The Lordship of Christ and Social Systems.*

Sheed & Ward
1-55612-013-3